There is no shortage of talk about the impact of the internet on democracy. Yet very little of this debate has seriously engaged with contemporary democratic theory. By developing an original theoretical framework for understanding new forms of communication and public participation, this book brings together previously insular perspectives in a way that both political theorists and communication scholars should welcome.

Kari Karppinen, *University of Helsinki, Finland*

Constrained Elitism makes a valuable contribution to the conceptualization of the liberal public sphere in relation to contemporary communicative practices. It offers a considered, informative, and persuasive account of how today's networked communications are helping to shape relationships between and amongst elites and non-elites within liberal democratic political systems. The central contribution of the book is to provide a general model of how networked communications are on the one hand enhancing the self-organizational capacity of publics, with the effect of increasing the pressure on elites by non-elite groups to address the latter's concerns, and on the other hand providing a means for advancing the competitive advantage of particular elites.

Lincoln Dahlberg, *University of Queensland, Australia*

Constrained Elitism and Contemporary Democratic Theory

Today, examples of the public's engagement with political issues through commercial and communicative mechanisms have become increasingly common. In February 2012, the Susan G. Komen Foundation reversed a decision to cease funding of cancer screening programs through Planned Parenthood amidst massive public disapproval. The same year, restaurant chain Chic-fil-A became embroiled in a massive public debate over statements its President made regarding same-sex marriage. What exactly is going on in such public engagement, and how does this relate to existing ideas regarding the public sphere and political participation? Is the public becoming increasingly vocal in its complaints? Or are new relationships between the public and economic and political leaders emerging?

Timothy Kersey's book asserts that the widespread utilization of internet communications technologies, especially social media applications, has brought forth a variety of new communicative behaviors and relationships within liberal polities. Through quick and seemingly chaotic streams of networked communication, the actions of these elites are subject to increasingly intense scrutiny and short-term pressure to ameliorate or at least address the concerns of segments of the population. By examining these new patterns of behavior among both elites and the general public, Kersey unearths the implications of these patterns for contemporary democratic theory, and argues that contemporary conceptualizations of "the public" need to be modified to more accurately reflect practices of online communication and participation.

By engaging with this topical issue, Kersey is able to closely examine the self-organization of both elite and non-elite segments of the population within the realm of networked communication, and the relations and interactions between these segments. His book combines perspectives from political theory and communication studies and so will be widely relevant across both disciplines.

Timothy Kersey is part-time Assistant Professor of Political Science at Kennesaw State University. He received his Ph.D. in political science from Indiana University in 2011. His research interests include contemporary democratic theory, comparative political behavior, and the social and political effects of technology.

Routledge Advances in Democratic Theory
Edited by David Chandler and Paulina Tambakaki
(both University of Westminster)

Advisory Board: Benjamin Barber (City University of New York), Rajeev Bhargava (Centre for the Study of Developing Societies), Bhikhu Parekh (House of Lords), Fred Dallmayr (University of Notre Dame), John Keane (University of Sydney), Chantal Mouffe (University of Westminster).

CENTRE FOR THE
STUDY OF
DEMOCRACY

Democracy is being re-thought almost everywhere today: with the widespread questioning of the rationalist assumptions of classical liberalism, and the implications this has for representational competition; with the Arab Spring destabilizing many assumptions about the geographic spread of democracy; with the deficits of democracy apparent in the Euro-zone crisis, especially as it affects Greece and Italy; with democracy increasingly understood as a process of social empowerment and equalization, blurring the lines of division between formal and informal spheres; and with growing demands for democracy to be reformulated to include the needs of those currently marginalized or even to include the representation of non-human forms of life with whom we share our planet.

Routledge Advances in Democratic Theory publishes state of the art theoretical reflection on the problems and prospects of democratic theory when many of the traditional categories and concepts are being reworked and rethought in our globalized and complex times.

The series is published in cooperation with the *Centre for the Study of Democracy*, University of Westminster, London, UK.

1. Nations and Democracy
   New theoretical perspectives
   Amanda Machin

2. Reclaiming Democracy
   Judgment, responsibility and the right to politics
   Edited by Albena Azmanova and Mihaela Mihai

3. Performing Citizenship
   Social movements across the globe
   Edited by Inbal Ofer and Tamar Groves

4. Constrained Elitism and Contemporary Democratic Theory
   Timothy Kersey

Constrained Elitism and Contemporary Democratic Theory

Timothy Kersey

NEW YORK AND LONDON

First published 2016
by Routledge
711 Third Avenue, New York, NY 10017

and by Routledge
2 Park Square, Milton Park, Abingdon, Oxon OX14 4RN

Routledge is an imprint of the Taylor & Francis Group, an informa business

© 2016 Taylor & Francis

The right of Timothy Kersey to be identified as author of this work has been asserted by him in accordance with sections 77 and 78 of the Copyright, Designs and Patents Act 1988.

All rights reserved. No part of this book may be reprinted or reproduced or utilized in any form or by any electronic, mechanical, or other means, now known or hereafter invented, including photocopying and recording, or in any information storage or retrieval system, without permission in writing from the publishers.

Trademark notice: Product or corporate names may be trademarks or registered trademarks, and are used only for identification and explanation without intent to infringe.

Library of Congress Cataloging in Publication Data
A catalog record for this book has been requested

ISBN: 978-0-415-72712-9 (hbk)
ISBN: 978-1-315-85563-9 (ebk)

Typeset in Sabon
by Taylor & Francis Books

Printed and bound in the United States of America by Publishers Graphics, LLC on sustainably sourced paper.

To Julia and Xander

Contents

List of illustrations   xii
Acknowledgement   xiii

   Introduction   1
1 Two Approaches to Elite Dominance   4
2 A Theory of Constrained Elitism   30
3 The Contemporary Networked Public Sphere   51
4 Constraint in the Networked Public   88
   Conclusion   118

Index   121

Illustrations

Figures

1.1 The Public-Elite Feedback Loop	14
3.1 Mediated and Networked Relationships	60
3.2 Conventional Public Output Processes	74
3.3 Networked Output Processes	77
4.1 Modeling Public Demands	90

Tables

3.1 Levels of Production in the Networked Public	57
4.1 Regulation of Elite Behaviors	95

Acknowledgement

This project emerged from concepts developed during the writing of my doctoral dissertation, so I must first thank my committee members, Dr. William Scheuerman, Dr. Russell Hanson, Dr. Aurelian Craiutu and Dr. Ted Striphas for their ideas, comments and support during the dissertation process.

I would also like to thank the Department of Political Science and International Affairs at Kennesaw State University for having me as a part of their faculty community over the past few years.

Additionally, this project would not have been completed without the patience and guidance of Natalja Mortensen and Lillian Rand at Routledge.

Most importantly, I would like to thank my wife Charity for her continuous support, feedback, and encouragement throughout the writing process.

Introduction

In January 2012, massive internet protests and public complaint led to the demise of two controversial pieces of legislation aimed at regulating online intellectual property. Throughout the summer and fall of the same year, quick serve restaurant Chic-fil-A became embroiled in a massive public debate over statements regarding same-sex marriage made by its President, Dan Cathy. Public consternation over the display of the Confederate Battle Flag on the grounds of the South Carolina capital reached a head in 2015, resulting in its official removal.

Such examples of the public's engagement with political issues appear to be increasingly common, especially through new means of communication, such as social media and mobile apps. In such examples, however, the public may not necessarily be participating in political processes or engaging in deliberative processes in the manner more conventionally associated with traditional conceptualizations of political agency.

Rather, these represent examples of the public *reacting*. The public reacts to events, such as natural disasters or school shootings. The public reacts to statements made by opinion leaders and decisions made by elected officials. Sometimes, it seems as though there is a public reaction to everything, no matter how insignificant.

So what, exactly, is going on with such public reactivity? One potential explanation is that the public has *always* been reactive; only now, the public's reactions are being amplified through the internet and social media. Another potential explanation is that the contemporary public has become more sensitive, more reactive, and more capable of voicing its discontent. Yet another explanation is that new relationships are beginning to emerge, both between the public and economic and political leaders, as well as among individuals within the public itself; within such new relationships, the public has developed a new sense of empowerment and entitlement which is expressed through reactivity.

All of these potential explanations hold some merit, yet none seem to fully represent the dynamic nature and significance of public reactivity. This book presents the argument that the widespread utilization of networked communications technologies, especially social media applications, has brought forth new behaviors and relationships within liberal polities. More specifically, the availability and ease of use of tools of networked communication create a social space in which clusters of individuals with shared interests, grievances, or normative commitments can form, effectively providing the public with a greatly increased capacity for self-organization. With such an enhanced capacity, individuals can find other individuals who care about the same issues as they do, or are suffering from the same problems as they are; while such interconnections may not be equivalent to a more conventionally understood community, they may nonetheless be meaningful or provide some degree of validation for individuals.

Individuals within the contemporary public thus voluntarily place themselves within networks of connections to like-minded persons; it is through such networks that the public's existing tendency to (negatively) react to external stimuli is accelerated and amplified. Through the rapid and seemingly chaotic streams of networked communication, the actions of political and economic elites are subject to increasingly intense scrutiny. The occurrence of some action or statement that runs contrary to the shared interests and commitments of such groups leads to the rapid mobilization of the public's ire and the creation of intense pressure to ameliorate or at least address the concerns of segments of the population.

This, however, is only the perspective of the public. From the perspective of elite actors, the public's reactive nature can be relied upon. In various forms of competition for status positions, elected offices, or simply for a good reputation, elite actors must be able to prompt and avoid public reactivity—to wield it against opponents like a club or ride upon it like a current of air. The same networked communications which allow the public to partially organize itself also enable elite actors to more strategically use the public for competitive advantage.

This book examines such interrelated processes and behaviors between elite actors and the public, with a particular emphasis on the means through which one layer is capable of structuring the actions and behaviors of the other. Chapter 1 provides a general introduction to the concept of elites and elite dominance by examining two broad approaches to understanding relationships between elite and non-elite layers of society. These two approaches—termed "elite realism" and "elite liberalism"—reflect broad understandings of the functional necessity and normative desirability of a stratified political system. Both approaches emphasize concepts conventionally located within the discipline of political science: the elite-realist approach focuses on the role of elites within electoral and policy-making processes, while the elite-liberal approach examines the role of elites in deliberative and discursive processes. Consideration of both approaches illustrates the competitive nature of the elite layer and the generally passive nature of the public layer.

Chapter 2 explains an alternative approach to elite dominance—termed the "multipolar" approach—derived from the concepts of French sociologist Pierre Bourdieu. Under this approach, the composition of the elite layer and the nature of its internal processes are conceived more broadly than the elite-realist or elite-liberal approaches; rather than focus on politically-oriented processes, the multipolar approach reflects a more holistic understanding of social action in which elite actors from a variety of fields struggle over multiple forms of social power. Building upon this approach, this chapter introduces the concept of elite constraint—the capacity of the public to set boundaries of acceptability on the actions and behaviors of elite actors—and specifically examines four broad categories of mechanisms of constraint available to the public.

Chapter 3 focuses primarily on the changing relationships between the public and elite layers of society which have been structured, in part, by changing communications technologies and practices. Traditional conceptualizations of "the public" need to be modified to more accurately reflect contemporary practices of online communication and participation, as well as the changing dynamics of elite/non-elite relations. This modification can be achieved by differentiating between two substrata of the public, referred to as "the general public" and "the intermediate public."

Chapter 4 provides an in-depth model of the relationships between the communicative activities of the intermediate public and the competition within elite segments. The nature of the interplay between processes of elite competition and constraint within the networked public are further illustrated by miniature case studies of numerous contemporary public events/controversies.

1 Two Approaches to Elite Dominance

Introduction

An uncommon event occurred in late 2014, when a fairly sophisticated piece of academic writing captured the attention of multiple national media outlets. In "Testing Theories of American Politics," Martin Gilens and Benjamin Page presented an empirical analysis of policy outcomes in the United States which suggested that the preferences of economically powerful individuals and interest groups are more significant than the preferences of average citizens.[1] While asserting the facticity of elite dominance is not noteworthy in itself, this article was seen as something of an innovation for using quantitative analysis for a conventionally normative topic. Beyond its potential impact as a work of social science, Gilens and Page's article was highly significant for the amount of attention within commercial and social media it generated. The idea that the American political system was not egalitarian, and perhaps *not even democratic*, moved outside of the realm of conspiracy theory or paranoia and into mainstream political discourse.

While the response to Gilens and Page's article is only anecdotal, it is nonetheless a powerful example of the resonance of the idea of elite dominance within the American public sphere. Questions of accuracy notwithstanding, a sufficient portion of the populace accept elite dominance as *real enough* to think about and discuss in the same manner as other political issues. That such considerations of the legitimacy of the political system itself became a part of the public agenda suggests an increased relevance, both within scholarly and non-scholarly communicative fora, to seriously examine the relationships between the elites and non-elite strata of contemporary American democracy.

As will be examined throughout this book, elites are conceptualized and differentiated from non-elites in multiple ways, an exhaustive review of which is outside of the intended scope of this project. Instead, what follows in this chapter is a structural model of two broad approaches to the role of elites within democratic polities as found within the disciplinary tradition of political science. The first approach, termed *elite-realism*, holds that the concentration of political power by an elite political class is both naturally occurring and necessary for the proper functioning of democratic systems; this approach primarily views elite actions through the lens of institutionalized elections. The second approach, termed *elite-liberalism*, emphasizes the need for elites to guide and assist the public in opinion-formation and decision-making processes; within this approach, elites primarily operate within the realm of public discourse. Each approach offers a different explanation of the relationship between elites and non-elites within the overall functioning of the political system; however, both share a similar assessment of the undesirability and/or impracticality of mass political participation. The following sections examine these two approaches, with a particular emphasis on the capacity of the (non-elite) public within the political process.

Electoral Competition and the Elite-Realist Approach

Beginning in the early twentieth century, numerous works of political, social, and economic scholarship examined the applicability of the "classical theory" of democracy to contemporary western societies. The classical theory of democracy, characterized by an assertion of the normative ideal of popular self-governance through highly responsive representative structures, was heavily scrutinized by such diverse theorists as Joseph Schumpeter, Walter Lippmann, Max Weber, V.O. Key, among many others. The various alternative perspectives to the classical theory offered by such scholars are commonly described as elitist in some manner (e.g. the elite theory of democracy, democratic elitism). The term *elitist* in this sense is not necessarily pejorative, but rather descriptive, as such theories explain the functioning of democratic systems not in reference to concepts such as the "common good," or the "will of the people," but rather to the concentration of decision-making power in a small subset of the population. Despite the broad range of arguments and normative commitments of the authors discussed in this section, their common acceptance of the empirical facticity of rule by a limited political class creates a shared quality of methodological realism, and can thus be seen as existing within a broad category of an elite-realist approach.

From the elite-realist perspective, large-scale political participation is unnecessary, if not undesirable. Whether through mechanisms of direct or representative democracy, citizens should play a minimal role within political decision-making processes, leaving the complex work of governing to more seasoned political actors. The only real responsibility of citizens is to vote regularly, exercising their capacity to affirm or negate their support for elected leaders. This limited role of citizens within the political system is not necessarily a function of disdain for the common person, but instead is justified on functional and psychological sets of arguments.

According to the elite-realist perspective, democratic political institutions function more effectively without excessive involvement from citizens. This is due in no small part to the complexity of political decision-making within large, modern polities; the degree of detail and quantity of information needed for rational considerations of law and regulation within contemporary societies is too great for ordinary citizens. Instead, it is only through experience and the assistance of policy experts that professional political actors can attempt to make the best governing decisions possible within any given context. For such experts and political agents, the opinion of the public is only marginally useful. According to Lippmann, public opinion only indicates the general sentiments of citizens; it cannot produce actual decisions regarding workable executive political action.[2] Similarly, Schumpeter argues that citizen participation outside the context of elections is an unnecessary distraction for political leaders, akin to "back-seat driving." Attempts by the public to continuously guide their representatives through highly participatory activities, such as the "practice of bombarding [legislators] with letters and telegrams," ultimately detract from the effectiveness of the democratic process by restricting the ability of elected officials to act freely.[3]

Weber provides a similar argument for professionalized, experienced political actors through his examinations of the modern state. The highly organized nature of the political system creates distinctions between elected political officials and administrative officials within state bureaucracies. Over time, as bureaucracies amass specialized knowledge regarding specific policy areas, the relative power of administrative officials increases within the political system. In the face of such bureaucratic power, even seasoned political actors appear as "'dilettantes" in regards to actual policy management, according to Weber.[4] Successful direction of the modern bureaucracy towards public ends (rather than towards its own ends) requires constant monitoring by a sufficiently experienced and independent parliament; the kind of intense oversight necessary to keep bureaucracy in check simply cannot be performed through mechanisms of mass democracy or public opinion.[5]

In addition to such functional arguments for the limiting the political power of citizens, the elite-realist approach holds that aspects of human psychology make mass participation inherently problematic. Elite-realists affirm that individuals are inherently rational, but that such rationality does not extend to the political realm. Instead, according to Schumpeter, individual rationality develops through praxis, as the consequences of decisions made within an individual's immediate sphere of life and activity are directly felt. As problems, decisions, and consequences become increasingly distant from daily life, they are further outside of the reach of individual reason, making opinions highly susceptible to prejudice, manipulation, or misinformation.

In relation to national politics, individual behavior ceases to appear even remotely based in rationality; the population, according to Schumpeter, is "incapable of action other than a stampede" within the electoral realm. When in groups, people are "terribly easy to work up into a psychological crowd and into a state of frenzy in which attempt at rational argument only spurs the animal spirits."[6] To the extent that any true will of the people exists, the public itself is incapable of articulating it; as Lippmann writes, "the making of one general will out of a multitude of general wishes is not an Hegelian mystery, as so many social philosophers have imagined, but an art well known to leaders, politicians and steering committees."[7]

The elite-realist perspective places a similar emphasis on limitations on the behaviors of members of the political class as well. Elites, according to Schumpeter, must demonstrate "democratic self-control" for the proper functioning of the political system. Such self-control comes in two forms: patience and temperance. As a characteristic of democratic self-control, patience is manifest in the willingness to let the inherently slow democratic process take its time; legislators should refrain from hasty decision making or manipulating parliamentary procedures for temporary advantages. Likewise, minority parties should be temperate in their behavior towards the majority group or party; all elites, whether in or out of power, must uphold the integrity of the democratic process by honoring the outcomes:

> ... the democratic method cannot work smoothly unless all the groups that count in a nation are willing to accept any legislative measure as long as it is on the statute book and all executive orders issued by legally competent authorities.[8]

This need for a shared culture of self-control underscores the importance of the existence of a distinct political class—one in which there is both a consensus on and commitment to democratic norms.[9] While such norms and limitations are effectively self-imposed by the political class, the threat of losing power through institutionalized competitive elections serves as an effective external restraint.

Under the elite-realist approach, the public has minimal responsibility within the political system; citizens should vote regularly, and leave the rest to whoever wins. This act of voting itself, however, is not necessarily a function of expressing the general will of the population, but rather a mechanism required to prevent collusion among the members of the political class. So long as there are more putative members of the political class than actual positions of power, elites will remain in competition for the public's electoral support. This general process of elite competition works in the following manner.

First, existing elite actors recruit more persons for positions within the political class (elected officials, party leaders, bureaucrats, etc.). Having a sufficiently large corps of quality potential political agents is necessary, according to Schumpeter, to meet the political system's need for "human material." The self-recruiting nature of the political class is also significant as a means of guaranteeing the talents and professional qualities of its members. Ideally, political careers would be made available only to those who have proven their capacity for good judgment as well as their commitment to democratic norms within other realms of society (e.g. through private sector or civic organizations). Due to such self-selection, citizens are effectively unable to pick their political leaders for themselves; in this sense, voting is a passive choice amongst a pre-selected slate of candidates, rather than an active choice of representatives.

Second, through voting and public opinion, citizens express approval or disapproval to existing political actions and elected officials. Again, in this regard, the public is passive and reactive; Lippman describes this limitation of the public as such:

> But in governing the work of other men by votes or by the expression of opinion they can only reward or punish a result, accept or reject alternatives presented to them. They can say yes or no to something which has been done, yes or no to a proposal, but they cannot create, administer and actually perform the act they have in mind.[10]

The public thus does not control or guide members of the political class in any meaningful way, but rather "aligns" itself with political actors on a particular side of public issues. Over time, political decisions become stabilized as the public simply ceases to express disapproval over specific issues.

The public's capacity to align with specific political actors is highly significant for understanding the strategic nature of elite competition. Given its normally passive nature, the public can only be mobilized through the initiative of existing members of the political class; by dramatizing and personalizing policy issues, elite actors can attempt to win the public to their side, creating an incentive for elite actors to attempt to manipulate the public's sentiment. The length to which any one elite actor can influence the public in this manner, however, is limited by the existence of other competing actors; should any political actor exceed the bounds of acceptable behavior based on the shared norms of the elite class, another actor would certainly use such violation of the public's trust to mobilize the public against them.

Under conditions of normal politics, the public remains in this passive mode, aligning itself with various political actors based on temporary concerns. According to Lippmann, this passivity exists even in the presence of abuse of political power; the public will wait for a challenge from a competing elite actor to express its grievances through alignment. Only when such abuses create crises or disruptions of everyday life, will the public itself become "aroused at evil."[11]

This shift in the behavior of the public from passivity during normal politics to *reactivity* during disruptive periods or crisis politics suggests at least a slight possibility that the public is capable of some kind of initiative beyond simple alignment with competing elites. This possibility becomes even more interesting, as the fundamental arbiter of what constitutes a disruption of everyday life is, in fact, the public itself. Given this, to the extent that the public (or partial segments of the public) becomes increasingly sensitive to disruption, the likelihood of spontaneous rejection of elite actions by the public increases as well. As will be argued later in this chapter, contemporary networked communications technologies may be such a mechanism for both increasing the public's sensitivity to elite actions, and for articulating its dissatisfaction.

Liberalism, Elites, and the Enlightenment

While the elite-realist approach provides a generally pessimistic assessment of the capacity of the public, the elite liberal approach sees the public as possessing a latent capacity for rationality. From this perspective, elites exist not to lead an ignorant or apathetic public, but to guide the public through the process of enlightenment. Such guidance occurs primarily through the exchange of arguments and ideas within the public sphere. Stripped to its basic Kantian roots, this elite-liberal approach holds that over time, the exchanges between scholars or other learned persons presenting their arguments on various collective issues before the public (presumably in written form), help steer the public towards the more effective use of reason. Through such actions, society is slowly transformed from an "age of enlightenment" into an "enlightened age."[12,13]

One means of spreading enlightenment is for the public to follow rational and deliberative examples set by elites in government. According to Jeremy Bentham, public access to the discourses of representative leaders can serve as such a means of both spreading rationality and socializing civic values; through publicity within legislatures, reason and a respect for good argumentation are promoted within the citizenry. By emulating parliamentary discourses, "[a] habit of reasoning and discussion will penetrate all classes of society. The passions, accustomed to a public struggle, will learn reciprocally to restrain themselves..."[14]

Similarly, this idea of guiding the public has been historically relevant for news media and the journalistic field. Under the "social responsibility" theory of the press, the legal and civic privileges which the press enjoys (e.g. special legal protections for journalists, access to broadcast spectrum) come at the cost of a special responsibility to provide quality information to the public and to serve the public interest. In the context of media regulation, "the public interest" is not merely a concept, but also a legal standard utilized by the Federal Communications Commission and the U.S. Supreme Court. Though fairly ambiguous, service of "the public interest" has been considered in the granting and renewal of broadcast licenses since the passage of the Federal Radio Act of 1927.[15] Amid concerns of expanded government regulation of the media through the public interest standard, *Time* publisher Henry Luce and University of Chicago President Robert Maynard Hutchins convened a panel of academics to evaluate the role of the press within modern democracies and effectively establish industry guidelines for self-regulation in the public interest.[16]

Published in 1947, the concluding report of the Hutchins Commission outlined five basic criteria which helped define the public service orientation of professional journalists. Responsible journalism would (1) provide factually accurate and contextually relevant information, (2) facilitate (rather than foreclose) continued public discussion of issues, (3) reflect constituent social groups (i.e. non-exclusionary), (4) clarify social values and goals, and (5) provide "full access to the day's intelligence."[17] These five substantive criteria, combined with the vision of the press as the facilitator of public enlightenment and watchdog of government, form the core of the social responsibility theory of the press as articulated by Theodore Peterson. Where the libertarian theory of the press held a core assumption that the public's desire for truth would animate good judgment in information seeking, the social responsibility theory holds that the public *needs the assistance* of civic-minded journalists.

Beyond merely a functional distribution of labor in the information-seeking process, the social responsibility theory suggests a moral duty for individuals to be informed and to make reasonable decisions in matters involving collective outcomes. However, as the use of reason is inconvenient for the public, members of the press have a responsibility to steer the public away from prejudice or indifference. According to the social responsibility theory:

> If man is to remain free, he must live by reason instead of passively accepting what he sees, hears, and feels. Therefore, the more alert elements of the community must goad him into the exercise of his reason. Without such goading, man is not likely to be moved to seek truth. The languor which keeps him from using his gift of reason extends to all public discussion. Man's aim is not to find truth but to satisfy his immediate needs and desires.[18]

Thus, in addition to the social responsibility to make rational and informed decisions, the press has a social responsibility to act as public trustees, guiding and informing the public in its decision-making.[19]

Habermas and "Considered" Public Opinion

The ideal of the public being led through rational-discursive processes by elite opinion leaders (e.g. public intellectuals, journalists) finds its most comprehensive articulation in Habermas' writings on the public sphere. The central theoretical issue for Habermas is the structuring of a public sphere in which public discourse is accessible for all members of the public, while also being sufficiently rigorous to promote and improve the public's rationality. In *The Structural Transformation of the Public Sphere* (STPS), one of his earliest and most widely critiqued texts on the public sphere, Habermas examines the emergence of the bourgeois public sphere in the eighteenth century, and its subsequent decline in the face of social transformation. In contrast to the relative discursive freedom found in the bourgeois public sphere, the contemporary public sphere lacks a true capacity for enlightenment and critical discourse.

This capacity of the public to think critically was reduced in part by the commodification of cultural goods; as markets for cultural goods broadened to meet the demands of an increasingly large and educated middle class, the complexity of cultural goods decreased. Works of art and literature could be comprehended and enjoyed by larger portions of the population, but at the cost of decreased opportunities for cultural goods to serve as common reference points for critical and social reflection. Newspapers and political journalism underwent a similar transformation; in commodity form, information and argumentation slowly merges with literature and entertainment (e.g. human interest news), thus ceasing to serve critical discourse. The intellectual demands on the reading public were further diminished by the widespread usage of comics, illustrations, and photography to convey news information (which Habermas refers to as the "American" model).[20]

In addition to reducing the need for critical reflection upon cultural goods and political information, commodification transformed the social context of consumption. Within the bourgeois public sphere, acts of private consumption (e.g. reading at home) induced acts of sociability via semi-institutionalized group meetings for "convivial discussion" of works. Contemporary commodity forms of cultural goods (e.g. films, radio), however, are already contained within a "noncommittal" social context; there is inducement towards neither sociability nor additional discussion. Not only does this echo the previously discussed passivity induced by overly accessible works, but also suggests that under conditions of commoditized information and cultural goods, the capacity of "the public" to organize itself as an institutional counterweight to the state is substantially reduced, if not altogether absent.[21]

Similarly, Habermas explains the shift from a "culture-debating" public to a "culture-consuming" public as involving an increased "administration" of conversation. Under mass-mediated communication, the interpretation of cultural goods and political news and information becomes absorbed into the production process itself. Debates over the meaning of a particular work or the significance of new developments on public issues are effectively prearranged into opposing issue positions which foreclose the possibility of compromise or consensus. The public, trapped within the confines of such administered discourse, ceases to possess either the structural or psychological capacity to formulate their own critical discourses; this creates, according to Habermas, a kind of "tutelage" wherein the public becomes dependent upon the prepared content of the media system.[22]

Habermas' invocation of Kantian terminology makes the point of his discussion of massification extremely clear: whereas the bourgeois public sphere represented the Kantian ideal of a cosmopolitan realm of individuals exercising their public reason, and in so doing, serving to further the advancement of enlightenment, the culture-consuming public *undermines* the enlightenment project by making the public increasingly dependent upon the prepared content of the media system.

This pessimistic assessment of the contemporary public in *STPS* invited a great deal of both favorable and critical analyses; in his own commentary on the work in the essay "Further Reflections on the Public Sphere," Habermas affirmed its radical-democratic orientation (i.e. actions of the state are legitimized only via processes of discursive will formation by an independent public, rather than economic or administrative interests) while signaling dissatisfaction with its methodology. In response to the criticism that his initial study overlooked the critical capacity of a pluralistic mass public, Habermas suggests that his initial pessimistic articulation of the "culture industry" argument, inherited from Adorno and Horkheimer, was overstated. Rather, with mass-mediated societies, the structuring and management of public opinion-formation is offset to the extent that public communication operates independently and spontaneously. According to Habermas, the ideally functioning public sphere requires a "spontaneous flow of communication unsubverted by power" within a non-organized communications environment "that is not geared toward decision making but toward discovery and problem resolution."[23]

More recent public sphere works by Habermas have attempted to further this inquiry into more feasible conceptions of the capacity of the public sphere. Where 1992's *Between Facts and Norms* focused on the role of civil society organizations in public communication, "Political Communication in Media Society" (*PCMS*) explores the internal structure and external relations of the media system.[24] In a clear demarcation from the "culture industry" arguments articulated in previous works, the model of the public sphere in *PCMS* no longer portrays the mass-media system as an impediment to deliberative processes. Rather, the mass-media system is portrayed as a mechanism for facilitating large-scale deliberative processes under certain conditions.

Central to *PCMS* is the subtle shift from *deliberation* to *deliberative processes* as the normatively desirable (and realistically achievable) goal within public communication. Having seemingly abandoned the more "demanding" expectations for individuals within the general public to participate in face-to-face deliberation within the general public, Habermas reconceptualizes the "deliberative model of democracy" to require the systematic and rational conversion of raw public attitudes or sentiments into "a plurality of considered public opinions." Understood as such, mass communication represents a means for "'laundering' flows of political communication" between the institutional discourses of the political system and the informal and mostly unstructured communication in civil society.[25]

Assuming all components function properly, the political public sphere thus resembles a kind of feedback loop comprised of a series of interactions between media actors and the general public. First, the public "senses" issues of collective concern as they emerge in the lifeworld through informal discourse and civil society organizations. Second, public elites (public actors and media professionals) "absorb impulses from civil society," contributing to the informal construction of a public agenda. Based on this agenda, public actors – politicians, party officials, lobbyists, and advocates and experts from civil society – present "published opinions" as contributions to public discourse. Third, the media structures an "elite discourse" by framing the issues and packaging the various published opinions, along with relevant contextual information into issue positions. Fourth, the public, having been exposed to published opinions of political actors, the reworked issue positions presented by the media, as well as the various mobilizations of preliminary public feedback (e.g. survey data), begins to develop "considered public opinions." Finally, these considered public opinions are re-articulated to both the political system and the elites within the public sphere through the various mechanisms of public opinion research.

Thus, through this feedback loop, the fairly wild range of reactive or non-reflective opinions become condensed into "a pair of contrary, more or less coherent opinions" which "express what appears, at the time, in the light of available information, to be the most plausible or reasoned interpretations of a sufficiently relevant – though generally controversial – issue." Within this cyclical opinion-formation process, the division of labor between the general public (i.e. the audience) and elite actors in the media system places most of the responsibility for formation of opinions on the public elites; members of the everyday public play a role *only* "if they manage to grasp the main lines of a... more or less reasonable elite discourse and adopt more or less considered stances on relevant public issues." According to Habermas, this minimal requirement can easily be assumed, as contemporary research into democratic engagement suggests that reasonable opinion positions form over long-term periods, after individuals are exposed to political information multiple times across differing contexts.[26]

Throughout *PCMS*, Habermas expresses a cautious optimism that the media system and the public *can* operate in the manner he describes; such optimism, however, is contingent upon the general public's capacity to act in a sufficiently responsive and self-reflective manner. Specifically, the general public must perform three activities. First, the public must arbitrate the recognition of elite public actors. Elite actors exist in all sectors of the lifeworld (e.g. the political system, the economic system), obtaining such positions through a variety of qualities; however, power obtained outside of the eyes of the public does *not* immediately convert into public influence. Instead, recognition of being an elite actor within the realm of public communication—being worthy of some degree of epistemic deference regarding issues of collective concern—requires a sufficient accumulation of "social" or "cultural" capital, which can only be evaluated and recognized by the public itself. The capacity of the public to extend or withdraw recognition

14 Two Approaches to Elite Dominance

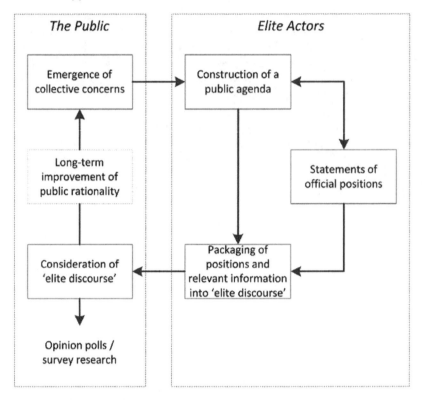

Figure 1.1 The Public-Elite Feedback Loop

or acclamation to elite public actors is an essential, as it serves to legitimize the epistemic deference upon which the remainder of the feedback loop rests.

Second, the public must follow the issue-based discourses which occur between elite public actors. "Following" in this context contains two meanings, each encoding a set of expectations of the public. On the one hand, the mass audience must simply pay attention, and attempt to "grasp the main lines of a ... more or less reasonable elite discourse." On the other hand, the public must "follow" elite discourse to the extent that it avoids straying from the range of issues and arguments presented before it.

Finally, the public must adopt "considered public opinions" on the issues identified as relevant and articulate those opinions through the relevant mechanisms of political input (e.g. voting, public opinion polls). Considered public opinions thus represent a narrowed range of articulations of agreement and disagreement, which serve to both "fix the parameters for the range of possible decisions which the public of voters would accept as legitimate," and provide "points of orientation for voters who can decide between competing platforms and programs."[27]

This model of the public sphere as a feedback loop between an independent media system and a responsive and reflexive public represents a notable break from Habermas' previous works—a movement which yields something closer to a successful empirically grounded articulation of a discourse-based normative theory of contemporary democracy. In this section, I identify two main points of departure between *PCMS* and previous iterations of Habermas' public sphere theory which generally serve to clarify significant concepts and relationships.

First, Habermas' explanation of the legitimacy of public actors represents a vast improvement over that of previous works. In *Between Facts and Norms (BFN)*, Habermas distinguished between two paths towards gaining recognition as a public actor worthy of epistemic deference. On the one hand, actors may *appear before* the public by mobilizing power and resources acquired in the political or economic systems; actors operating in this manner attempt to instrumentally affect public discourse through various mechanisms of public relations. Actors appearing before the public are suspect, as their visibility and putative authority are buttressed by resources and processes of organizational power which lie outside of the view (and involvement) of the general public.[28] On the other hand, actors who *emerge from* the public gain authority and visibility through the "indigenous" formations of civil society organizations; as such associations (e.g. churches, non-profit organizations) represent institutionalized extensions of the general public itself, actors in leading roles within civil society possess an inherent quality of acquired authenticity.[29]

As constructed in *PCMS*, however, this kind of public authenticity—additionally referred to by Habermas as social or cultural capital—represents a *continuous variable* which corresponds to an actor's accrued "capital" of public recognition or acceptance. This movement away from *BFN*'s binomial classification of *appearing before* and *emerging from* is not merely a semantic change, but a rejection of the antagonism between authenticity and the mechanisms of public relations. Simply stated, in the contemporary mass-mediated public sphere, all participants *appear before* the public to some degree, irrespective of the authenticity of the content of their messages. Successful communication requires some utilization of the mechanisms of public relations, which technological developments and market forces have placed within the means of nearly all potential public actors; for actors and organizations within the public sphere, being media savvy is no longer incompatible with being authentic. Given that all public actors must ultimately gain and maintain some form of acceptance before the public, media relations seems to be an inevitable activity for even the most genuinely public interested groups.

Thus within *PCMS*, appearing before the public through the utilization of media or public relations represents "strategic interventions in the public sphere," which Habermas accepts as simply part of the process of public opinion formation.[30] What makes such strategic intervention relatively benign is the assumption (carried over from *BFN*) that "Public opinion can be manipulated but neither publicly bought nor publicly blackmailed."[31] In the final instance, the authenticity or legitimacy of public actors *and* the content of public discourse is determined by its acceptance by the diffused audience of the public itself. *When* such evaluation occurs, and *what happens* when the public withdraws acceptance represents the second main point of departure from previous works.

As presented in *Between Facts and Norms*, the public itself is generally dormant; during periods of normal politics, the development of authentic public discourse is thwarted by various pathologies of mass communication, not the least of which are the tendencies towards non-critical discourse and market dependency in the mass media. Despite such impediments, the interests of the public *can* be articulated through the mechanism of civil society organizations; problems in the lifeworld are detected by the associations and organizations which constitute the "civil-social periphery" and re-articulated to the institutions of the political system. This power of civil society, however, only truly emerges during times of crisis or extraordinary politics; in such times, when pressing collective issues are left unresolved through "the systemic inertia of institutional politics," the public's capacity to generate political pressure becomes activated.

While the revised model presented in *PCMS* suggests no revisions to the civil-social periphery's role during periods of crisis politics, it does depict a slightly less dismissive function of the public itself during normal politics. Whereas in *BFN*, everyday (i.e. non-crisis) processes of public opinion formation are routinized and non-critical, in *PCMS*, they form the basis for reflexive opinion formation. By continuously monitoring the outputs of the media system, the public is actively engaged in a constant motion of formation and re-formation of public opinion.

Such continuous monitoring and engagement, however, may have an adverse impact on public discourse to the extent that the public becomes distracted in its opinion formation process. As discussed in the following section, such problems may be exacerbated by the quantity and speed of information flows enabled by networked communications technologies.

The Networked Public and its Problems

Within the past few decades, the widespread utilization of networked computers for communicative applications (i.e. internet communications technologies, or ICTs) has brought about extensive social, political, economic, and cultural changes. The capacity for groups and individuals to communicate with each other has increased dramatically, substantially altering the landscape in which information is produced and consumed. In addition to changes in the infrastructure of communications, new behaviors and practices of communication have emerged. Individuals use social networking applications to share information and interact with a wide variety of other individuals within thin personal networks. Commenting on and redistributing media has blurred the line between production and consumption of media information. The sum of these structural and cultural changes is often referred to as a shift from a mass-mediated public sphere to a networked public sphere.[32]

This change from mass-mediated to networked forms of communication is not simply a shift in technological applications (i.e. from television to internet), but also of different sets of organizing principles. Mass-mediated communications processes generally reflect "top-down" processes through which information streams are created by a limited number of producers and sent to a wide audience.[33] In contrast, networked communications processes reflect a many-to-many principle, whereby nearly anyone with internet access and basic computer skills can act as an information producer for a seemingly infinite audience.

Such changes in both the technological capacities of mass communication and the habits and practices of communication they facilitate create new issues for the overall functioning of the public within democratic systems; two such issues—levelling and value socialization—are of particular relevance for the larger consideration of the capacity of the public.

Junk Thought and the Levelling of Communication

One of the more powerful effects of networked communications technology is a tendency towards leveling in many forms of online communication.[34] Simply stated, both the ease of attaining a speaker or producer position within public communication (that is to say, being the source of a communicative act in some form) and the sheer number of speakers within public communication make differentiation simultaneously more necessary and more difficult to achieve. Underlying this critique is the assumption of the normative desirability of a limited number of speaker positions within communicative relationships, as only a limited number of persons possess the necessary skills to make meaningful contributions to public discourse. Such an elite-directed public sphere does not exclude everyday citizens, but rather conditions non-elite participation to be mostly passive and indirect.[35]

In *The Cult of the Amateur*, Keen observes this flattening of communicative positions as a shift in the relative perceptions of experts and amateurs within the networked public sphere. According to Keen, enthusiasm for the networked public confounds the relationship between expert and amateur in two ways. First, the values of democratization, inclusion, and equalized access and participation are mistakenly seen as being universally applicable and functional; while these values are indispensable for the functioning of the democratic political sphere, when exported into the realm of knowledge and cultural goods production, such production begins to malfunction.[36] Second, the expert/lay relationship has been skewed by the myth of the "noble amateur." Amateurs in the networked public sphere are viewed as a corrective to the problems created by specialization of knowledge: where professionalization leads to conformity and bounded thinking, amateurs are inherently more diverse and free to "think outside the box"; where experts' actions within their relevant institutional structures are motivated by the preservation and furtherance of their careers, amateurs are motivated by passion, and free of institutional restraints.

The primary effect of the rise of the amateur, according to Keen, is the fall of the expert. While this devaluation of expertise and professionalism has had tremendous economic consequences for nearly all cultural production industries (e.g. publishing, films, music), its effects on the general health of the public sphere are best seen in the realm of journalism.[37]

The rise of the amateur manifests itself within the realm of journalism in the form of bloggers and citizen journalists. Heralded by technology enthusiasts as an alternative to the commercialized and risk-averse mainstream media, bloggers and citizen journalists do not seek to become part of the system of professional journalism, but rather make a deliberate effort to exist outside it. As described by Barbara Kaye in her study of bloggers' motivations and self-identifications vis-à-vis mainstream media:

> [B]log users are primarily attracted to blogs because of the unique characteristics of blogs. Users perceive that bloggers present information in ways that cannot be found elsewhere. For example, users like blogs because bloggers keep a story going, they admit their bias up front, they outscoop traditional media, they provide links to other sources, they provide in-depth and insightful commentary and analysis perceived to be absent from other media and they are not filtered or censored by traditional media gatekeepers.[38]

The high standards and discriminating practices associated with top professional media outlets are seen not as the source of institutional credibility, but rather as a form of fascism of ideas.[39] However, by eschewing the institutional aspects of professional media—editing, proofreading, fact-checking, corroboration—the products of citizen journalism tend more towards opinion and gossip than real investigative journalism.[40] It is perhaps telling that some of the most notable examples of blogs and citizen journalists are instances of political scandal rather than sustained investigation; the Drudge Report's breaking of the Lewinsky scandal in 1998 and the mobilization of political pressure against Trent Lott following his remarks regarding Strom Thurmond's segregation-era Presidential campaign are frequently heralded by blog enthusiasts as instances of the success of new media.[41] More often, however, blogs resemble diaries and anthologies of opinions, rather than independent works of journalism.[42]

Returning to the issue of value socialization, the privileging of amateurism within the networked public can be seen as the negation of the values of commitment and long-term achievement. Expert or professional status does not simply appear out of nowhere, but rather is earned:

> Becoming a doctor, a lawyer, a musician, a journalist, or an engineer requires a significant investment of one's life in education and training, countless auditions or entrance and certifying exams, and commitment to a career of hard work and long hours. A professional writer spends years mastering or refining his or her craft in an effort to be recognized by a seasoned universe of editors, agents, critics, and consumers, as someone worth reading and paying attention to...[43]

Privileging the "noble amateur" thus represents a shortcut around the professionalization process—a denial of both the functional necessity and the intrinsic value of committed work towards the goal of professional certification. Keen sees this de-privileging of professionalization reflected in the intersection (or lack thereof) between professional culture and popular culture. In the "golden age of media," prominent journalists (e.g. Walter Cronkite, Edward Murrow) were seen as what Keen terms "cultural heroes," a position consisting of trust and respect, as well as recognition of career achievement. Both a person as the object of admiration and a position as the object of aspiration, such cultural heroes embody a set of values regarding hard work, respect, deference, and achievement. Contemporary public communication, however, has no such equivalent; the noble amateur replaces the professional journalist, and the celebrity replaces the cultural hero.

This contemporary de-privileging of expertise and professionalism is not surprising, given that the relationships between experts and intellectuals and the general public have frequently been portrayed as tenuous. Richard Hofstadter's argument that long standing anti-intellectualism within Anglo culture manifests itself as an egalitarian resentment of excellence seems eerily prescient of contemporary debates regarding the merits of amateur information production.[44]

The groundwork for the contemporary de-privileging of expertise and professionalism, however, cannot be entirely attributed to folk-wisdom trends within American culture, as the standards of excellence which buttress expertise and professionalism have at times been sacrificed by elites for their own benefit. According to Coser, the emergence of a college-educated middle class demanding more accessible forms of social sophistication led to the phenomena of the intellectual-as-celebrity. Coser describes the intellectual-as-celebrity as effectively bypassing "the arduous and complicated process through which other intellectuals attempt to gain recognition among qualified judges."[45] Instead, the intellectual-as-celebrity courts popularity from "an amorphous general public" which lacks the knowledge necessary to judge the value of any such contributions. Susan Jacoby's description of "junk thought" encapsulates a similar process wherein skewed arguments and pseudo-scientific data are utilized by "highly intelligent people to mislead and confuse a public deficient in its grasp of logic, the scientific method, and the basic arithmetic required to see through the pretensions of poorly designed studies."[46]

Within the contemporary networked public sphere, the public's simultaneously increasing capacity for choice and decreasing capacity of judgment/evaluation has led to increase in the promulgation of such "junk thought." The process of amateur-led and peer-based (i.e. non-professionalized) gatekeeping and distribution of information contribute to the spread of junk thought, as there are neither the mechanisms (e.g. professionalism, credential, and experience) nor the widespread disposition of individuals to evaluate the evidence associated with any particular claim. Given the choice among potentially authoritative sources of information, internet users—especially young ones—take little account of the actual source of information in evaluating political messages; individuals were equally likely to be convinced by information coming from celebrities as experts.[47]

Public controversies over the safety of vaccines serve as an illustrative example of both the promulgation of junk thought and, more specifically, the power of celebrity-experts. In 1998, a group of thirteen researchers led by Andrew Wakefield published a paper in British medical journal *The Lancet* which posited a relationship between MMR vaccination, gastrointestinal dysfunction, and autistic developmental disorders.[48] This paper, known colloquially as the "Wakefield report" caught the attention of mainstream media in Britain and the United States, prompting a public scare over safety of routine vaccinations.

After aggressive efforts by the medical community to calm the public, the debate over vaccine safety seemed to have gone dormant.[49] The controversy, however, was renewed in 2007 with the publication of comedienne and former model Jenny McCarthy's memoir, *Louder than Words: A Mother's Journey in Healing Autism*. McCarthy's controversial views on autism—that the development of autistic disorders is linked to ingredients in vaccines, and that special therapies and diets can help children autistic disorders[50]—were promoted and reproduced with little or no contextualization vis-à-vis the dominant views of scientific and medical communities on a number of major media venues (e.g. *Oprah, Larry King Live, ABC News*).

McCarthy's memoir focused primarily on her experiences raising and caring for her autistic son; during numerous promotional television appearances, the narrative advanced by McCarthy linked the onset of her son's symptoms with his receipt of routine MMR vaccinations.[51] In the wake of these appearances, McCarthy became an outspoken figurehead for a burgeoning anti-vaccination movement as well as an advocate for various holistic and non-traditional autism treatments, joining the organization *Generation Rescue* as board member and spokesperson. Undoubtedly due in part to McCarthy's activism, donations to *Generation Rescue* nearly tripled from $425,000 in FY2007 to $1.2 million in FY2008.[52]

Despite the preponderance of evidence against the MMR-autism link, a 2009 survey of parents conducted by health researchers at the University of Michigan found continuing support for the autism-vaccine link. 25% of respondents agreed with the statement "Some vaccines cause autism in healthy children." Additionally, 11.5% of respondents reported having refused physician-recommended vaccinations for their children, overwhelmingly citing concerns of adverse side effects.[53] Aside from the obvious effect of promoting junk thought—with potentially dangerous public health effects—celebrity "experts" risk diverting public attention away from pressing issues and towards their own pet projects.[54] In a communicative environment in which such failure to scrutinize the source and credibility of putative experts is not buttressed by the standards of professional journalism, few barriers to the popularization of junk thought exist.

Isolation and Fragmentation in the Public

An additional concern with the networked public sphere is that networked communications have a strong isolating and individualizing effect. Applications of internet communications technologies, especially those which facilitate customization of information exposure, place individuals at the center of their own communicative universe. Within internet communications, the individual is self-oriented in nearly all aspects: interlocutors and communicative communities are self-chosen, the distribution of content within information streams is self-chosen, the individual's own contributions to information streams (comments, video clips, social bookmarks, etc.) are invited at every occasion. It is with this spirit of individual empowerment that the magazine *Time* declared 2006's "Person of the Year" to be: YOU![55]

Such communicative egoism, however, comes at the cost of atomizing individuals and undermining social cohesion. As with the other phenomena discussed in previous sections, these problems of communicative egoism do not originate with applications of networked communication, but rather are amplified and accelerated by them. The communicative egoism which frequently occurs under networked communications acts as a centrifugal force, atomizing individuals and pushing them away from one another. At the interpersonal level, networked communications strip social relationships from the information production and distribution process. Under conditions of networked communication, the acquisition and production of knowledge ceases to be a social activity as individuals become (literally) nameless and faceless components of information streams—an information age version of Heidegger's standing-reserve.[56]

This form of alienation is not new to networked communications technologies; agrarian social critic and technology skeptic Wendell Berry identifies the weakening of interpersonal relationships as an unavoidable consequence of the innovation-to-obsolescence cycle of technological change. According to Berry, interpersonal relationships (familial relationships, within his specific example) come at the expense of technological development:

> It is well understood that technological innovation always requires the discarding of the "old model" – the "old model" in this case being not just our old Royal standard, but my wife, my critic, closest reader, my fellow worker. Thus what would be superseded would be not only something, but somebody. In order to be technologically up-to-date as a writer, I would have to sacrifice an association that I am dependent upon and that I treasure.[57]

Beyond interpersonal relationships, the individualizing effect of networked communications risks social cohesion through the customization of information exposure and interlocutors. Through such customization, individuals avoid the randomness associated with geographically structured associations, a phenomenon which Robert Wachbroit describes as the creation of "custom communities." As such custom communities consist of like-minded individuals involved by self-selection, there is a risk of non-exposure to diversity of opinion; without diversity, there is little opportunity or need for the inculcation of tolerance as a communicative value.[58] Furthermore, as communities within the networked public sphere are self-chosen, individuals holding opinions contrary to the implicit majority within a particular communicative forum have no requirement or incentive to attempt to change others' opinions: one either stays silent, or changes communicative venues.

To place this in Tocquevillian terms, customization of communities presents a situation in which the public sphere resembles an infinite number of small, insulated majority tyrannies. These do not pose a problem for discourse at the national level based on the Madisonian assumption that at a large enough aggregation, there will be ample communicative groups with opposing views, but rather for the inculcation of communicative values—or lack thereof. De Tocqueville's description of majorities in America is almost perfectly applicable to common experiences within online message boards:

> In America the majority draws a formidable circle around thought. Inside those limits, the writer is free; but unhappiness awaits him if he dares to leave them. It is not that he has to fear an auto-da-fé, but he is the butt of mortifications of all kinds and of persecutions every day.[59]

Thus, such custom communities condition individuals to tolerate majority tyranny—both in submission and in enforcement—as part of the normal way of things.

An additional problem of communicative egoism is a loss of commonly shared information exposure and conceptualization of common problems. In his 1995 book, *Being Digital*, computer scientist and early internet proponent Nicholas Negroponte introduced the concept of the "Daily Me"—electronically delivered news whose content and format were customized to the exact preferences of the individual recipient.[60] Beyond the practical problems of echo chambers (e.g. extremism), customized filtering of information exposure carries a number of normative risks; the desirability of the "Daily Me" has been thoroughly examined by legal scholar Cass Sunstein.

According to Sunstein, mass media outlets (e.g. newspapers, broadcasters) act as "general-interest intermediaries" by directing a range of topics, viewpoints, and arguments towards a wide, undifferentiated audience. In doing so, general-interest intermediaries act as a kind of public forum, exposing individuals to diverse content and—perhaps more importantly—creating "shared experiences for a heterogeneous public."[61] Such shared experiences are essential for the building and maintenance of solidarity and commonality in a diverse polity, acting as "a kind of social glue, facilitating efforts to solve shared problems, encouraging people to view one another as fellow citizens, and sometimes helping to ensure responsiveness to genuine problems and needs."[62]

In addition to shared experiences, general-interest intermediaries contain an element of randomness to individual media exposure which is (purposefully) missing from "Daily Me" customized media exposure. Such random (i.e. not pre-selected) media exposures provide individuals with information which may be of no use to themselves, but may be later shared with others. This sharing of information and larger conceptualization of information distribution as a collective responsibility helps to maintain the norms of trust and reciprocity within a diverse society.[63] To the extent that individuals use networked communications to seek information from specialized sources, rather than general-interest sources, the benefits of information sharing fail to materialize.

Such potential problems have not gone unnoticed. In one of his most pointed statements on the effects of networked communication, Habermas claims that "the welcome increase in egalitarianism brought to us by the Internet is paid for with the decentralization of access to unedited contributions. In this medium, contributions by intellectuals lose the power to create a focus."[64] Given the additional problems of amateurism, junk thought, and atomization, the role of elite actors within the elite-liberal framework becomes increasingly significant; elites must retain a capacity to guide the public's attention towards issues of significant common interest using sound argumentation and evidence.

Returning to Habermas, such guidance takes the form of a specific division of intellectual/information labor between elite public actors and the public itself. Opinion leaders within the public sphere (e.g. journalists) prepare the public for democratic decision-making by "selecting the matters which are relevant for political decision-making, reworking them into statements of problems and aggregating them into competing public opinions through more or less well-informed and reasoned arguments."[65] The public's responsibility is to pay close and considerate attention to such elite discourses and express their opinions through the relevant mechanisms (e.g. voting, opinion polls). Giving the task of reformulating or "laundering" the preferences of the general public to elite actors within public communication is intuitively pleasing, as elite public actors possess a greater capacity to rearticulate public demands before the political system. However, this division of labor releases the public from any requirement of possessing "autonomous moral self-discipline and civilized self-control" while simultaneously failing to induce any socialization processes through discourse.[66] The public must simply reflect upon and choose between rationally determined "yes" or "no" response packages produced by elite public actors, producing not necessarily consensus, but rather a narrowed range of inputs into the political system.[67]

According to Habermas' revised model, the feedback loop between the public and the public elite can result in the expression of reflexive (i.e. considered) public opinions; reflexivity, in this sense, refers to the public's opinion-formation process. Within the feedback loop, the public acts reflexively to the extent that they reconsider their own basic opinions in the context of "public opinion" as presented before it by elite public actors. Reflexivity thus requires a degree of political and communicative engagement on behalf of the public; individuals in the public need to actively monitor the outputs of elite public actors and reconsider their own views within broader social contexts.

Such requirements for engagement and consideration could seemingly be fulfilled via networked communications, particularly those practices which offer discursive opportunities with diverse interlocutors (e.g. blogs, bulletin boards). Additionally, by inviting more diverse forms of individual expression, elite-level actors would possess a greater capacity to ascertain the impulses and concerns of the public. Networked communications thus facilitate a more communicatively active public—both in terms of information seeking and elite-level feedback—which could potentially support the kind of reflexivity which Habermas claims to be necessary. However, to the extent that networked communications distract the public, they risk introducing fragmentation by countering the narrowing effect of elite public actors. Such questionable utility of an active networked public suggests an unresolved ambiguity in Habermas' conceptualization of the reflexive public: the public must actively monitor and consider the outputs of public opinion leaders, but not be so communicatively active as to work against the narrowing efforts of elite public actors.

Conclusion

Perhaps inadvertently, the requirement for the public to follow elite discourses necessarily generates market forces among elite public actors; elite public actors must not only establish themselves as being worthy of the public's recognition, but must also struggle to gain the public's scarce attention. Competition under the elite-liberal framework thus appears as a fluid corps of elite public actors continuously moving within a hierarchy of influence. Viewed in this manner, the strategic interventions into processes of public opinion formation by elite actors are, in effect, two-level games. On one level, elite actors situate themselves in relation to their audience through the content of their messages as well as the style and manner in which they are communicated. On the other level, elite actors must situate themselves in relation to each other, establishing their own authenticity and/or disputing that of their competitors.

By generating a competitive environment in this manner, the elite-liberal approach appears to have more in common with the elite-realist approach than would be seen at first glance. While the elite-realist approach emphasizes the competitive nature of elites, it is limited by a narrow understanding of politics as existing within electoral institutions. Similarly, the elite-liberal approach utilizes a broader understanding of politics as existing within discursive and communicative spaces, yet it underestimates the competitive nature of such public discourse. Therefore, what appears necessary is an alternative approach to competitive elite behaviors which utilizes a broader space of elite action, both in and outside of electoral institutions. Such an approach can be found in the writings of French sociologist Pierre Bourdieu and will be further examined in the following chapter.

Notes

1 Gilens and Page, "Testing Theories of American Politics."
2 Lippmann, *The Phantom Public*, 41–2.
3 Schumpeter, *Capitalism, Socialism and Democracy*, 295.
4 Weber, Gerth, and Mills, *From Max Weber*, 196.
5 Weber, *Economy and Society: An Outline of Interpretive Sociology*, 1456.
6 Medearis, *Joseph Schumpeter's Two Theories of Democracy*, 120. Schumpeter, *Capitalism, Socialism and Democracy*, 257–9.
7 Lippmann, *The Phantom Public*, 37.
8 Schumpeter, *Capitalism, Socialism and Democracy*, 294.
9 Dahl, *Who Governs?*, 320.
10 Lippmann, *The Phantom Public*, 41–2.
11 Ibid., 57–60.
12 Kant, "What Is Enlightenment?"
13 Habermas, *The Structural Transformation of the Public Sphere*, 103–5.
14 Bentham, *Political Tactics*, 31.
15 Coase, "The Federal Communications Commission." Caldwell, "The Standard of Public Interest, Convenience or Necessity as Used in the Radio Act of 1927."
16 Horwitz, "On Media Concentration and the Diversity Question," 181–2. Baker, "The Media that Citizens Need," 348–9. McIntyre, "Repositioning a Landmark: The Hutchins Commission and Freedom of the Press."
17 Siebert, Peterson, and Schramm, *Four Theories of the Press*, 87–91. Baker, "The Media that Citizens Need," 349.
18 Siebert, Peterson, and Schramm, *Four Theories of the Press*, 100.
19 Brants and de Haan, "Taking the Public Seriously: Three Models of Responsiveness in Media and Journalism," 416.
20 Habermas, *The Structural Transformation of the Public Sphere*, 166–70.

21 Ibid., 163.
22 Ibid., 164–71.
23 Habermas, "Further Reflections on the Public Sphere," 451.
24 Habermas, *Between Facts and Norms: Contributions to a Discourse Theory of Law and Democracy.*
25 Habermas, "Political Communication in Media Society: Does Democracy Still Have an Epistemic Dimension? The Impact of Normative Theory on Empirical Research."
26 Habermas, "Political Communication in Media Society," 416.
27 Ibid., 166–7, 172.
28 Habermas, *Between Facts and Norms: Contributions to a Discourse Theory of Law and Democracy.*
29 This directly relates to Peters' conception of public authority. See Peters, "On Public Deliberation and Public Culture."
30 Habermas, "Political Communication in Media Society," 419.
31 Habermas, *Between Facts and Norms: Contributions to a Discourse Theory of Law and Democracy*, 364.
32 Benkler, *The Wealth of Networks: How Social Production Transforms Markets and Freedom*, 10–13. See also Manuel Castells' *The Rise of the Network Society.*
33 Castells, *The Rise of the Network Society*, 359.
34 The terms "leveling" and "flattening" are used interchangeably in this section.
35 Ferree et al., "Four models of the public sphere in modern democracies," 290–2.
36 Keen, *The Cult of the Amateur: How Today's Internet is Killing Our Culture*, 15.
37 Ibid., 48–53.
38 Kaye, "Blog Use Motivations: An Explanatory Study," 141.
39 Leigh, "Are Reporters Doomed?"
40 Keen, *The Cult of the Amateur: How Today's Internet is Killing Our Culture*, 53.
41 Lessig, *Free Culture: How Big Media Uses Technology and the Law to Lock down Culture and Control Creativity.* Hewitt, *Blog: Understanding the Information Reformation That's Changing Your World*, 8–10.
42 Papacharissi, "Democracy online: civility, politeness, and the democratic potential of online political discussion groups," 35.
43 Keen, *The Cult of the Amateur: How Today's Internet is Killing Our Culture*, 63.
44 Hofstadter, *Anti-Intellectualism in American Life*, 51.
45 Coser, "The Intellectual as Celebrity," 47.
46 Jacoby, Susan, *Age of American Unreason*, 229.
47 Kaid and Postelnicu, "Credibility of Political Messages on the Internet."
48 Wakefield et al., "Retracted."
49 Fitzpatrick, *MMR and Autism: What Parents Need to Know.*
50 McCarthy and Carrey, "My Son's Recovery from Autism."
51 For description and additional media related to these appearances, see "The Oprah Winfrey Show (Sept 18, 2007): Jenny McCarthy and Holly Robinson Peete – Their Fight to Save Their Autistic Sons." and "Larry King Live (transcript: April 2, 2008)."
52 Tax filings data retrieved through GuideStar USA's nonprofit directory. GuideStar, "Nonprofit Report: GENERATION RESCUE."
53 Freed et al., "Parental Vaccine Safety Concerns in 2009."
54 West and Orman, *Celebrity Politics*, 113. For a defense of celebrity politics, see Street, "Celebrity Politicians: Popular Culture and Political Representation."
55 Grossman, "Time's Person of the Year: You."
56 Heidegger, "The Question Concerning Technology."
57 Berry, "Why I Am Not Going to Buy a Computer."
58 Wachbroit, "Reliance and Reliability: The Problem of Information on the Internet," 38.

59 Tocqueville, *Democracy in America*, 244.
60 Negroponte, *Being Digital*.
61 Sunstein, *Republic.com 2.0*, 31.
62 Ibid., 117. See also Buchstein, "Bytes that bite," 259–61.
63 Sunstein, *Republic.com 2.0*, 104–8.
64 Original text: "Der begrüßenswerte Zuwachs an Egalitarismus, den uns das Internet beschert, wird mit der Dezentrierung der Zugänge zu unredigierten Beiträgen bezahlt. In diesem Medium verlieren die Beiträge von Intellektuellen die Kraft, einen Fokus zu bilden." Habermas, "Ein Avantgardistischer Spürsinn für Relevanzen."
65 Habermas, "Media, Markets and Consumers: The Quality Press as the Backbone of the Political Public Sphere," 135–6. Habermas, "Political Communication in Media Society: Does Democracy Still Have an Epistemic Dimension? The Impact of Normative Theory on Empirical Research," 162.
66 This formulation of "responsible" action on behalf of individuals within a deliberative environment comes from Offe, "Bindings, Shackles, Brakes: On Self-Limitation Strategies," 43–5.
67 See Habermas' discussion of "yes" and "no" statements in Habermas, "Media, Markets and Consumers: The Quality Press as the Backbone of the Political Public Sphere," 162.

Bibliography

Baker, Edwin. "The Media that Citizens Need." *University of Pennsylvania Law Review* 147, no. 2 (1998): 314–408.

Benkler, Yochai. *The Wealth of Networks: How Social Production Transforms Markets and Freedom*. New Haven, CT: Yale University Press, 2006.

Bentham, Jeremy. *Political Tactics*. New York: Oxford University Press, 1999.

Berry, Wendell. "Why I Am Not Going to Buy a Computer." *Harper's Magazine*, May 1987.

Brants, Kees, and Yael de Haan. "Taking the Public Seriously: Three Models of Responsiveness in Media and Journalism." *Media, Culture & Society* 32, no. 3 (2010): 411–428.

Buchstein, Hubertus. "Bytes that Bite: The Internet and Deliberative Democracy." *Constellations* 4, no. 2 (1997): 248–263.

Caldwell, Louis. "The Standard of Public Interest, Convenience or Necessity as Used in the Radio Act of 1927." *Air Law Review* 1, no. 3 (July 1930).

Castells, Manuel. *The Rise of the Network Society*. 2nd edn. *The Information Age: Economy, Society, and Culture* 1. Malden, MA: Blackwell Publishers, 2010.

Coase, Ronald H. "The Federal Communications Commission." *The Journal of Law and Economics* 2 (1959): 1–40.

Coser, Lewis. "The Intellectual as Celebrity." *Dissent* 20 (1973): 45–46.

Dahl, Robert A. *Who Governs? Democracy and Power in an American City*. New Haven, CT: Yale University Press, 1989.

Ferree, Myra Marx, William A. Gamson, Jurgen Gerhards, and Dieter Rucht. "Four models of the public sphere in modern democracies." *Theory and Society* 31, no. 3 (2002): 289–324.

Fitzpatrick, Michael. *MMR and Autism: What Parents Need to Know*. London: Routledge, 2004.

Freed, Gary L., Sarah J. Clark, Amy T. Butchart, Dianne C. Singer, and Matthew M. Davis. "Parental Vaccine Safety Concerns in 2009." *Pediatrics* 125, no. 4 (March 2010): 654–659.
Gilens, Martin, and Benjamin I. Page. "Testing Theories of American Politics: Elites, Interest Groups, and Average Citizens." *Perspectives on Politics* 12, no. 3 (2014): 564–581.
Grossman, Lev. "Time's Person of the Year: You." *Time*, December 13, 2006. www.time.com/time/magazine/article/0,9171,1569514,00.html.
GuideStar. "Nonprofit Report: GENERATION RESCUE," n.d. www2.guidestar.org/organizations/20-2063267/generation-rescue.aspx.
Habermas, Jürgen. "Political Communication in Media Society: Does Democracy Still Have an Epistemic Dimension? The Impact of Normative Theory on Empirical Research." In *Europe: The Faltering Project*. Malden, MA: Polity Press, 2009.
Habermas, Jürgen. "Media, Markets and Consumers: The Quality Press as the Backbone of the Political Public Sphere." In *Europe: The Faltering Project*, 131–137. Malden, MA: Polity Press, 2009.
Habermas, Jürgen. "Political Communication in Media Society." *Communication Theory* 16, no. 4 (2006): 411–426.
Habermas, Jürgen. "Ein Avantgardistischer Spürsinn für Relevanzen." *Der Standard*. March 10, 2006.
Habermas, Jürgen. *Between Facts and Norms: Contributions to a Discourse Theory of Law and Democracy*. Cambridge, MA: MIT Press, 1996.
Habermas, Jürgen. "Further Reflections on the Public Sphere." In *Habermas and the Public Sphere*, edited by Craig Calhoun, 421–461. Cambridge, MA: MIT Press, 1992.
Habermas, Jürgen. *The Structural Transformation of the Public Sphere: An Inquiry into a Category of Bourgeois Society*. Studies in Contemporary German Social Thought. Cambridge, MA: MIT Press, 1991.
Heidegger, Martin. "The Question Concerning Technology." In *The Question Concerning Technology and Other Essays*, edited by William Lovitt, 3–35. New York: Garland Publishing, 1977.
Hewitt, Hugh. *Blog: Understanding the Information Revolution That's Changing Your World*. Nashville, TN: T. Nelson Publishers, 2005.
Hofstadter, Richard. *Anti-Intellectualism in American Life*. New York: Knopf, 1963.
Horwitz, Robert. "On Media Concentration and the Diversity Question." *The Information Society* 21, no. 3 (July 2005): 181–204.
Jacoby, Susan. *Age of American Unreason*. New York: Pantheon Books, 2008.
Kaid, Lynda Lee, and Monica Postelnicu. "Credibility of Political Messages on the Internet." In *Blogging, Citizenship, and the Future of Media*, edited by Mark Tremayne, 149–164. New York: Routledge, 2007.
Kant, Immanuel. "What Is Enlightenment?" In *The Portable Enlightenment Reader*, edited by Isaac Kramnick, 1–7. New York: Penguin Books, 1995.
Kaye, Barbara. "Blog Use Motivations: An Explanatory Study." In *Blogging, Citizenship, and the Future of Media*, edited by Mark Tremayne, 127–148. London: Routledge, 2007.
Keen, Andrew. *The Cult of the Amateur: How Today's Internet is Killing Our Culture*. New York: Doubleday, 2007.
"Larry King Live (transcript: April 2, 2008)," n.d. http://transcripts.cnn.com/TRANSCRIPTS/0804/02/lkl.01.html.

Leigh, David. "Are Reporters Doomed?" *The Guardian*. November 12, 2007. www.guardian.co.uk/media/2007/nov/12/mondaymediasection.pressandpublishing3?gusrc=rss&feed=media.

Lessig, Lawrence. *Free Culture: How Big Media Uses Technology and the Law to Lock down Culture and Control Creativity*. New York: Penguin Press, 2004.

Lippmann, Walter. *The Phantom Public*. New Brunswick, NJ: Transaction Publishers, 1993.

McCarthy, Jenny, and Jim Carrey. "My Son's Recovery from Autism." *Turner Broadcasting System*, April 2008. http://articles.cnn.com/2008-04-02/us/mccarthy.autsimtreatment_1_autism-evan-hannah-poling?_s=PM:US.

McIntyre, Jerilyn S. "Repositioning a Landmark: The Hutchins Commission and Freedom of the Press." *Critical Studies in Mass Communication* 4 (1987): 136–160.

Medearis, John. *Joseph Schumpeter's Two Theories of Democracy*. Cambridge, MA: Harvard University Press, 2001.

Negroponte, Nicholas. *Being Digital*. New York: Knopf, 1995.

Offe, Claus. "Bindings, Shackles, Brakes: On Self-Limitation Strategies." In *Modernity and the State*, 31–60. Cambridge, MA: MIT Press, 1992.

"The Oprah Winfrey Show (Sept 18, 2007): Jenny McCarthy and Holly Robinson Peete – Their Fight to Save Their Autistic Sons," September 18, 2007. www.oprah.com/showinfo/Jenny-McCarthy-and-Holly-Robinson-Peete.

Papacharissi, Zizi. "Democracy online: civility, politeness, and the democratic potential of online political discussion groups." *New Media & Society* 6, no. 2 (April 2004): 259–283.

Peters, Bernhard. "On Public Deliberation and Public Culture." In *Public Deliberation and Public Culture*, 68–118. New York: Palgrave Macmillan, 1997.

Schumpeter, Joseph A. *Capitalism, Socialism and Democracy*. London; New York: Routledge, 1943.

Siebert, Fred S., Theodore Peterson, and Wilbur Schramm. *Four Theories of the Press*. Freeport, NY: Books for Libraries Press, 1973.

Street, John. "Celebrity Politicians: Popular Culture and Political Representation." *British Journal of Politics and International Relations* 6 (2004): 435–452.

Sunstein, Cass. *Republic.com 2.0*. Princeton: Princeton University Press, 2007.

Tocqueville, Alexis de. *Democracy in America*. Translated by Harvey Mansfield. Chicago, IL: University of Chicago Press, 2000.

Wachbroit, Robert. "Reliance and Reliability: The Problem of Information on the Internet." In *The Internet in Public Life*, edited by Verna Gehring, 29–41. New York: Rowman & Littlefield, 2004.

Wakefield, A. J., A. Anthony, J. Linnell, D. M. Casson, M. Malik, M. Berelowitz, A. P. Dhillon, M. A. Thomson, P. Harvey, and others. "Ileal-lymphoid-nodual hyperplasia, non-specific colitis, and pervasive developmental disorder in children." *The Lancet* 351, no. 9103 (1998): 637–641.

Weber, Max. *Economy and Society: An Outline of Interpretive Sociology*. Edited by Guenther Roth and Claus Wittich. Berkeley: University of California Press, 1922.

Weber, Max, Hans Heinrich Gerth, and Charles Wright Mills. *From Max Weber: Essays in Sociology: Essays in Sociology*. Oxford: Oxford University Press, 1946.

West, Darrell, and John Orman. *Celebrity Politics*. Upper Saddle River, NJ: Prentice Hall, 2003.

2 A Theory of Constrained Elitism

Introduction

As discussed in the previous chapter, elite actors compete through a variety of mechanisms for various goals. Elites compete for the public's electoral support through the mechanism of regular popular votes, as emphasized by the elite-realist perspective. Elites also compete for authority status before the public, as emphasized by the elite-liberal perspective. Within such interactions between elite and public layers, the public takes a subordinate, if not entirely passive role; the general terms of the public's choices between candidates, opinion leaders, or sets of issue frames are determined at the elite level, rather than being structured by a fully autonomous public.

The passive nature of the public, however, poses little threat to the functioning of the democratic process, as an active citizenry is ultimately not necessary, as the elite realm is effectively self-regulating. Elite actors possess sufficient normative commitments to tolerance and self-control and appreciate the significance of these values for governing. Additionally, the ever-present threat of an electoral loss serves to keep the behaviors of elite actors in check.

Despite its inherent passivity, the public plays a highly significant role within the larger process of elite competition by possessing a capacity to *refuse* the choices being put forward by elites. Not unlike in Hegel's explanation of the master-slave relationship, elite actors *depend upon* public recognition to pursue their ends. Such recognition may take multiple forms: votes represent an institutional form of recognition for elected officials; opinion leaders find recognition through various metrics of media viewership. In accepting or rejecting the choices offered to it, the public exercises a capacity to grant, or more importantly, to *withhold* such recognition to elite actors.

As the realm of elite actions is ultimately self-directing, the public's ability to withhold or withdraw recognition from elite actors should not be mistaken for a form of *control*, but rather, as a form of *constraint*. While the public may not be able to direct the actions and behaviors of elite actors, by exercising its capacity of constraint, the public indicates which elite actions, behaviors, policies, decisions, etc. are considered unacceptable. Over time, discrete acts of constraint begin to constitute "boundaries" of acceptability, structuring (but not determining) the behaviors of elite actors as well as the larger competitive realm. This capacity of the public to constrain elite actors will be examined in more depth throughout this chapter, but it is first necessary to visit the issue of elite competition yet again, utilizing a broader conceptualization of the realm in which elite competition exists.

Multipolarity in Elite Competition

As previously discussed, the elite-realist and elite-liberal approaches depict different aspects of elite competition: the elite-realist approach places elite competition within the institutionalized spaces of politics, while the elite-liberal approach looks at competition within broader discursive spaces. Both of the approaches are correct, yet both only partially capture the dynamics of the elite realm.

Within both approaches, elite competition involves not only competition between individual actors, but also a struggle to establish the legitimacy of the existence of the elite layer itself. The issue of legitimacy is generally assumed to be a *non-issue* within the elite-realist approach, under the presumption that the electoral institutions themselves legitimize the asymmetrical relationship between representatives and constituents. Competition within the realm of public communication more clearly demonstrates the necessity of such legitimization; elite actors do not compete for votes, but rather for the legitimacy of their claims of deference and recognition.[1]

Elite competition thus involves two goals: the acquisition of some form of power (e.g. the political power of an elected office, power over public opinion), and the recognition of its legitimate existence and usage. The consideration of competition between elites is therefore inextricable from the differentiation between elite and non-elite segments of society. The concepts of French sociologist Pierre Bourdieu, in particular, those which explain multiple forms of capital and social power, are highly useful for further understanding the dynamics of elite competition and constraint within what can be termed a *multipolar* approach.

According to Bourdieu, one of the central limitations within contemporary social theory is an unquestioned dominance of the logic of economic theory (i.e. economism): human behaviors and potential individual actions are examined solely in terms of rational self-interest, and all forms of social exchange and interaction are understood as forms of market exchanges.

For purposes of understanding issues related to elite/non-elite differentiation, economism produces an overly limited conception of capital solely as economic resources; rather, capital should be understood broadly, as an accumulated force which allows its holders to "appropriate" other forces (e.g. the labor of others).[2] Certainly, economic material fits this description, as economic capital can accumulate, generate profit, or be exchanged for other resources; this, however, is not the only form of capital that exists to generate social power for its holder. Three additional forms—cultural capital, social capital, and symbolic capital—exist alongside economic capital as accumulated forces that serve to structure both the differentiation between elite and non-elite spaces, as well as the internal dynamics of the elite space itself.

Capital in its economic form is fairly straightforward: individuals and organizations objectively possess capital in the form of currencies, properties, natural resources, etc. The nature of possessing and acquiring economic capital is institutionalized through property rights and other various legal mechanisms. Economic capital is utilized through generally transparent exchanges, the totality of which constitutes "the economy" of any given society.

Cultural Capital

Cultural capital is less straightforward, both in terms of its visibility and its capacity for transparent exchange, as it represents a form of social power derived from primarily individual characteristics. Cultural capital exists in one manner as a set of dispositions or mores which reflect a long-term commitment to self-development towards certain competencies. Learning to read Latin, for example, would represent an effort to acquire cultural capital; while there may be some functional benefit for reading Latin in specific contexts (e.g. medical and legal professions), the true gain comes from having demonstrated the desire for knowledge and self-improvement for their own sake as well as the discipline sufficient for its fulfillment. In other words, cultural capital comes not from *knowing* Latin, but from *having learned* Latin.

In this manner, cultural capital exhibits a curious relationship with economic capital. Acquiring cultural capital through such self-development represents a negation of economic capital; learning skills which directly manifest themselves in terms of gaining economic capital (e.g. corporate executives learning to speak Mandarin in order to improve relations with Chinese partners) do not necessarily signify a desire for self-cultivation. As nearly anyone is capable of pursuing their material self-interest, acquiring new ways of gaining economic capital does not signify any real distinctiveness of one's character. Furthermore, the long-term nature of developing cultural capital necessarily represents an investment of time and resources that might otherwise be put towards material gains. Acquiring cultural capital thus requires some degree of renunciation or transcendence of immediate economic interests.

At the same time, individuals must possess a certain level of economic capital to be able to pursue cultural capital; learning to read Latin requires a certain amount of leisure (e.g. non-work) time as well as sufficient access to necessary resources (e.g. books, language programs). While some economic capital is required, it cannot be directly converted into cultural capital; paying for an expensive language course is not enough, one must make the commitment to actually doing the work of learning to gain cultural capital.

Cultural capital may also exist in a more external, objectified form though academic achievements and qualifications. Primarily reproduced through the educational system—particularly through the differentiation between elite and non-elite schools—individuals acquire cultural capital by having been accepted into and graduated from prestigious educational institutions. The actual accomplishments or educational performance of an individual are only marginally important; so long as the institution itself remains prestigious and selective, its graduates acquire cultural capital under the assumption that they have been sufficiently socialized towards self-cultivation. The existence of institutional sources of cultural capital is absolutely necessary, as they create a barrier between elite and non-elite segments of the social world that *cannot* be surmounted by individual effort; the holder of a *Juris Doctorate* from a highly rigorous and well regarded publically funded school will never be considered the equivalent of a graduate of the Harvard Law School. Hierarchies of prestige among elite schools also serve to create a common metric for comparison of cultural capital among elite actors. Thus, in the same way that some elites may compete based on economic wealth (e.g. the number of homes owned), others may compete through institutionalized cultural capital (e.g. my children attend a highly selective preparatory school).

Social Capital

Memberships within groups and networks may also be a resource in the form of social capital. While social capital may not necessarily manifest itself in objective forms, it is nonetheless highly significant in nearly all societies. The flows of information, opportunities, and resources throughout the social whole are neither arbitrary nor neutral in nature, but rather occur within networks of interpersonal sociability. An actor's standing within such networks represents their social capital. Like the other forms of capital, social capital represents a long-term investment; social actors must work to maintain their status by maintaining interpersonal relationships (e.g. attending class reunions) and expanding their network connections.

For the social whole, social capital is highly significant for the maintenance of elite/non-elite distinctions, by creating and reinforcing in-group/out-group status differentiation. The lack of social capital, in particular, has a paralyzing effect on the upward mobility of putative elites; not knowing the right people, not being invited to the right parties/events, not having notable personal references, etc., serve to maintain the exclusivity of the elite realm. In this manner, social capital is highly related to cultural capital to the extent that educational institutions additionally serve as social institutions; however, institutionalized cultural capital does not guarantee social capital. To maintain their in-group status, social actors must continuously demonstrate their embodiment of specific group norms as well as the generically sociable values such as reciprocity and solidarity.

As social capital exists primarily through relationships, it is unsurprising that familial relationships are highly significant for its acquisition and transmission. Social capital can be transmitted through parentage, as evidenced by the social power of influential family names (e.g. Kennedy, Bush, Rothschild) as well as the institution of hereditary peerage; similarly, social capital can be transmitted or acquired through marriage. As with cultural capital, social capital often exists alongside economic capital, but it cannot be outright purchased; social capital only accrues to those whose manners and actions demonstrate worthiness of in-group status.

In itself, the conceptualization of capital as a variety of forms of resources is not entirely complicated; rather, the greater significance of Bourdieu's arguments comes in regard to the relations between the forms of capital. Generally speaking, the three forms of capital are interchangeable. Various mechanisms exist through which quantities of one form of capital can be converted into another; such conversions, however, are not without limitations.

Of the three forms of capital, economic capital has the greatest capacity for conversion. As mentioned in the previous discussions, economic capital can be converted to cultural capital across generations; middle-class parents "invest" their economic capital in tuition at selective schools, private cello lessons, or study abroad programs with the hope of future cultural capital dividends for their children.

Economic capital can similarly be converted into social capital fairly easily; through the mechanism of philanthropy, in particular, social inclusion and importance can effectively be purchased with charitable giving. Conversion in the reverse direction, however, is much less likely, as the fruits of labors towards self-cultivation and the maintenance of social relationships are illiquid in nature.

Symbolic Capital

While the possession of economic capital makes the acquisition of social and cultural capital possible, it cannot do so in a direct and transparent manner. The objective marks of cultural and social capital (e.g. a degree from a prestigious school) cease to be mechanisms of distinction between class layers to the extent that they are seen as commodities. Instead, there must be some intermediation which hides the facticity of the use of economic power to gain cultural and/or social power. This, according to Bourdieu, is the function of symbolic capital.

Social practices based on the outright use of power (especially in the form of economic capital) for the immediate gain of its holder cannot reinforce the distinctions between elite and non-elite social layers. All individuals, regardless of their location within the hierarchies and divisions of the social whole, can act in a self-interested manner, and recognize such behaviors in others; as such, self-interested actions are, by definition, not distinctive. The self-interested use of economic power is, therefore, somewhat ironically, a great social equalizer. Perhaps more importantly, the self-interested use of economic power almost always involves some degree of exploitation. Such exploitation exists in a range from the physical and violent (e.g. slavery, human trafficking) to barely perceptible differences in exchange values; even in voluntary, mutually beneficial exchanges among rough equals, one party will always "get a better deal" than the other.[3]

The self-interested use of economic power, as well as the larger system of economic exchanges in society, thus becomes tainted by exploitation, be it real or perceived, brutal or gentle. In order to actually utilize their potential power, holders of economic capital must possess an additional resource—symbolic capital—which serves to legitimize their actions. In its most basic articulation, symbolic capital can be understood as a kind of reputation; those who possess symbolic capital are perceived as having some kind of positive, unique, or distinctive personal qualities which neutralize any suspicion of exploitation (e.g. they are honorable and fair, they possess integrity, they have a genuine commitment to a cause, etc.).

Symbolic capital can thus be understood as the negation of economic capital. As social actors must use their labors for the expansion of their economic, social, or cultural capital, they must also engage in symbolic exchanges which actively deny economic self-interest. Bourdieu uses the example of gift-giving to demonstrate the parallel logics of symbolic capital and economic capital. Gift-giving requires that for the symbolic exchange to be valid, both parties must deliberately refuse the logic of price and calculation; should the values of gifts be openly compared, the practice itself becomes empty and meaningless.

More significant, however, is the net effect of the gift exchange for both parties when there is a notable asymmetry of values. If Serena gives Clemont a high value item and receives a low value item in return, Serena has effectively suffered an economic loss. However, Serena has simultaneously increased her symbolic capital to the extent that she is viewed as generous by Clemont and all others witness to the exchange. Through repetitions of such exchanges, especially if done in a conspicuous manner, Serena's symbolic wealth may eventually reach a critical mass wherein her generosity ceases to be a simple character trait, and instead forms the basis for symbolic power. Serena's choice of who receives gifts as well as the choices of the gifts themselves are imbued with a kind of "magical" power: any gift that Serena gives *must be* special or valuable; anyone who receives a gift from Serena *must be* favorable in some manner.

While this is a rudimentary example, it nonetheless serves to illustrate the process through which economic capital, disguised by symbolic capital, becomes a form of power whose use is recognized as legitimate and non-exploitative. This symbolic power (i.e. disguised economic, cultural, or social power) gives its holder a capacity to manipulate the symbolic order through which the social world is understood. Bourdieu writes:

> [S]ymbolic power has to be based on the possession of symbolic capital. The power to impose upon other minds a vision, old or new, of social divisions depends on the social authority acquired in previous struggles. Symbolic capital is a credit; it is the power granted to those who have obtained sufficient recognition to be in a position to impose recognition.[4]

Capital, Classes, and Struggle

Given the multiple forms of capital, as well as their complex interrelations, class distinctions based on ownership and labor are ultimately insufficient. Instead, Bourdieu conceptualizes the social whole as a "multi-dimensional space of positions" based on the relative volume and distribution of capital contextually possible.

On the one hand, social actors are distributed by the total volume of capital they have accrued; although it is effectively a continuous variable, the total volume of capital cannot be used to demarcate classes in an empirical sense. Nonetheless, the interrelated nature of the different forms of capital does tend to create similarities of practices and interests at each level that resemble classes. Within the lowest level—what is functionally equivalent to a "working class"—practices demonstrate a kind of "poverty cycle" wherein cultural and social capital cannot be accrued due to a lack of the necessary surplus economic capital. The lack of social and cultural capital leads to limited educational and occupational opportunities, culminating in an overall incapacity for upward mobility. The highest level effectively constitutes an elite or dominant class; actors within this space possess significant amounts of all forms of capital. The space in-between these two extremes represents a kind of middle class, whose members possess a limited total volume of capital. Actors within this space may possess some capacity for upward mobility, but are otherwise excluded from entering or competing with the dominant class.

Social actors may also be differentiated on an *intra-class* basis by "the relative weight of the different kinds of capital in the total set of their assets."[5] Different positions within classes possess different combinations of capital and thus develop differing, if not outright antagonistic, interests in regard to increasing their total volume of capital. Intra-class differentiation thus induces a level of competitiveness between different positions within the dominant layer. Bourdieu writes:

> In advanced societies, one of the fundamental problems arising at the heart of the field of power is that of the harmonious articulation of the

diverse forms of capital that stand in objective competition with each other—making intellectuals accept that they are intellectuals and not managers, making managers consent to becoming managers by renouncing being intellectuals. For what has to be reproduced is a system of differences which defines a historically given division of the work of domination.[6]

The elite space within the social whole is thus characterized by multiple forms of competition, both at the individual level, as actors labor to maintain or increase their total capital, and at the group level, where various subgroups (e.g. intellectuals, artists, business leaders) attempt to improve their position within the dominant space vis-à-vis other groups. Such competition, however, must be partially attenuated, as actors in the dominant layer must simultaneously act in a collusive manner, so as not to disrupt or weaken inter-class boundaries.

Elite intra-class competition therefore finds its ideal form in the struggle for symbolic power, as this struggle necessarily involves the maintenance of forms of distinction, of social divisions, and ultimately of domination. Elites of all subgroups utilize the forms of capital they possess in a struggle to improve their reputation and to expand the scope of their recognition. Such a struggle is ultimately a contest between forms of capital (or compositions of capital) for the greatest legitimacy and most efficient conversion into power over the symbolic order, and thus, over the social whole. To the extent that one form of capital dominates other forms across elite subgroups, its legitimacy extends across class layers as well, becoming what Bourdieu refers to as the "dominant principle of domination."[7]

Public Policy and Elite Competition

Competition *within* the various fields of the social whole is to be readily expected; competition *across* fields, however, is less straightforward. Actors possessing different compositions of capital and operating within different fields are unlikely to have opportunities to compete directly, as each field has its own distinct formulations of economic and symbolic capital. Respect within the business community, for example, cannot be readily compared to respect within the scientific community, or to rank in the military, or to esteem within the art world, etc. Competition within the realm of public policy, however, solves this problem of incomparability.

Actors from nearly all elite subspaces (e.g. business leaders, media personalities, civic groups, scientists) have a potential capacity to influence the formation of public opinion and public policy. The realm of political communication, opinion-formation, and decision making thus becomes a common game, within which all forms of capital may be employed. The reward for the "winners" of this game is the temporary and limited usage of the apparatus of the state to generate some competitive advantage within the elite realm. While such usage *may* involve the state's capacity for legitimate violence, within advanced societies, the true value of the state lies with its capacity for manipulation of symbolic order.[8] Bourdieu describes the stakes of this "game of politics" as:

> on the one hand, the monopoly of the elaboration and diffusion of the legitimate principle of division of the social world and, thereby, of the mobilization of groups, and, on the other hand, the monopoly of the use of objectified instruments of power (objectified political capital). It thus takes the form of a struggle over the specifically symbolic power of making people see and believe, of predicting and prescribing, of making known and recognized, which is at the same time a struggle for power over the "public powers" (state administrations).[9]

At this point, a clearer and more comprehensive understanding of competition within the elite realm emerges; elites across multiple sectors (or fields), utilizing various combinations of forms of capital, compete for the ability to utilize the capacity of the state for manipulation of the symbolic order. The legitimacy of nearly all social practices—actions, behaviors, relationships, identities, etc.—may be granted or denied through the apparatus of the state, thus structuring perceptions and recognizable claims of domination, exclusion, and exploitation.

Examples of the legitimizing power of the state are fairly abundant. More recently within American electoral politics, concerns regarding wealth inequality have become increasingly visible. During the 2012 presidential election primaries, such concerns informed a series of criticisms of Republican candidate Mitt Romney regarding his federal taxes. Tax information made publically available by Romney, whose professional background consisted of both political and business/financial sector experience, documented an effective tax rate of 15.6% in 2011—a rate lower than the national average effective rate of 18%, and significantly less than the highest nominal rate of 35%.[10] While Romney's tax disclosures themselves generated minor scrutiny within political media, they were more significant as a proxy for struggle over diffuse perceptions of unfairness in tax policy—specifically, that taxing investment income at a lower rate than ordinary (i.e. wage-based) income represents a form of economic injustice. A variety of arguments regarding the economic rationality of these different rates were advanced on behalf of Romney and the larger investment/financial system. Romney himself, however, advanced a particularly interesting defense during a Republican Party debate, saying: "I pay all the taxes that are legally required and not a dollar more. I don't think you want someone as the candidate for president who pays more taxes than he owes."[11] Constructed as such, concerns regarding the fairness or legitimacy of the rates paid by Romney (and presumably, others with similar financial contexts) are moot, as the rates are inherently legitimized by the state. Moreover, full utilization of economic advantages within the tax system represents a virtue; individuals whose sense of fairness or propriety or justice motivates a refusal to extract tax advantages are not just economically irrational, but also *unfit* for holding elected office. As illustrated by this line of argumentation, the legitimizing power of the state is virtually unassailable; the use of any advantage codified in law, regardless of how unfair it may be perceived to be or what disadvantages may result from it, should be not only *permitted*, but *lauded* within the social whole.

Obergefell v. Hodges – Struggle over the Symbolic Order

In June 2015, the United States Supreme Court announced its decision in *Obergefell v. Hodges*, which held that states were required to grant and recognize same-sex marriage licenses under the 14th Amendment to the U.S. Constitution. As a function of the legal system, this change can best be described as resulting from an institutional mechanism of constraint. The case, however, must also be understood as the end point of a decades-long struggle for the symbolic legitimacy of homosexual persons—a struggle which has involved nearly all aspects of the social whole, slowly becoming part of normalized political competition.

For purposes of this project, the *Obergefell* case itself illustrates the significance of the state apparatus for structuring the social order; interestingly, however, this is best seen through the dissenting opinions of the Supreme Court Justices in the voting minority. Specifically, the arguments presented in dissenting opinions by Chief Justice John Roberts and Associate Justice Antonin Scalia depict the majority decision as a form of domination by articulating the Court's symbolic legitimacy in terms of judicial restraint.

According to Roberts, American citizens:

> are in the midst of a serious and thoughtful public debate on the issue of same-sex marriage. They see voters carefully considering same-sex marriage, casting ballots in favor or opposed, and sometimes changing their minds. They see political leaders similarly reexamining their positions, and either reversing course or explaining adherence to old convictions confirmed anew. They see governments and businesses modifying policies and practices with respect to same-sex couples, and participating actively in the civic discourse. They see countries overseas democratically accepting profound social change, or declining to do so. This deliberative process is making people take seriously questions that they may not have even regarded as questions before.[12]

Contestation over same-sex marriage thus illustrates the healthy functioning of the republican structure of government; constituencies of both issue camps (i.e. those for or against same-sex marriage) use social, economic, and institutional means to express their views and shape American society through a kind of Madisonian political praxis. These processes of democratic self-articulation are ultimately realized through the works of legislatures—especially those of the states. As such, the institutional capacity of the Supreme Court to dominate political processes (through powers of judicial review and judicial supremacy) is legitimate to the extent that it shows *deference* to legislatures. The role of the judiciary, from this perspective, is not to be a mechanism for social change, but simply for the resolution of legal inconsistencies or ambiguities. By issuing a decision which represents "an act of will, not legal judgement," the majority justices have exceeded the boundaries of proper self-limitation and unnecessarily foreclosed political debate on this issue.

Roberts' dissent is particularly interesting in its frank discussion of the state's power over the symbolic order. The capacity for the state to structure the ordering of society is taken as a given, with seemingly no interest in concealing this power of domination. Rather, the primary theoretical concern is how such symbolic manipulation becomes legitimate. The majority opinion's appeals to transcendent values of equality, dignity, and autonomy to legitimize their decision are insufficient, as they are ultimately subjective evaluations. Instead, symbolic interventions can only be valid when such value judgments are made *by the people themselves* and realized through legislative processes.

Constructed as such, concerns regarding domination become moot, as there is no differentiation between the will of the people and the outputs of legislatures; the usage of the apparatus of the state for acts of symbolic manipulation *cannot* be understood as a form of domination when the people themselves have authorized and enacted it. Instead, by virtue of refusing to defer to legislatures, the majority justices are engaged in acts of domination. As Justice Scalia writes:

> to allow the policy question of same-sex marriage to be considered and resolved by a select, patrician, highly unrepresentative panel of nine is to violate a principle even more fundamental than no taxation without representation: no social transformation without representation.[13]

This example thus serves as a useful illustration of the nature of competition over the symbolic powers of the state within the elite realm.

Elite actors seeking to use or direct the apparatus of the state must do so in a manner which conceals their immediate interest in doing so. Rather, elite actors must appear *disinterested*—their actions must be perceived as being motivated by something other than their own benefit or will to power; failure to do so would make elite actions appear as domination and jeopardize the stability of elite/non-elite distinction. Democratic institutions lend themselves nicely to the depiction of such disinterest through the common referent of "the people," making a construction of "the people" and a means for acting on its behalf an essential component of all elite action. In this example, Roberts and Scalia construct the will of the people as being represented through legislatures, with deference to legislatures representing an ideal form of disinterested behavior. After establishing one's own disinterestedness, effective competition requires the additional step of attempting to negate the symbolic legitimacy of your opponents by claiming that *their* actions are motivated by self-interest, rather than the disinterested enactment of the will of the people.

In regard to such controversial issues, the state's capacity for symbolic violence is apparent. Once an issue position has been made "official," those of the opposing position find their beliefs rendered invalid or unaccepted among the larger social whole, and will likely be subject to intense pressure for conformity. As such, elite actors competing over controversial issues may not try to occlude the facticity of symbolic violence, but instead, to place the responsibility for it on the opposing camp. The sometimes frustrating logic of the political game, in which strategies of blaming and name calling appear effective, may thus be necessary for the perpetuation of the elite/non-elite distinction overall.

Four Mechanisms of Elite Constraint

Through such struggles over both the actual policies of the state and the perceptions of the policies of the state, elite actors seek to increase the relative volume and/or legitimacy of their capital, while simultaneously structuring and reinforcing distinctions between elite and non-elite layers of the social whole. However, within democratic polities, such struggles *necessarily* involve the public to some degree; while the symbolic powers of the state may be directed by elite actors, such directions *cannot* contradict the democratic principles—consent of the governed, political equality, etc.—on which the state's legitimacy rests. As such, elite competition within the public realm introduces a variety of opportunities for individuals outside of the elite realm (i.e. everyday citizens) to influence elites by constraining their behaviors.

Through their support, both through electoral mechanisms and within broader public discourse, members of the public empower elite actors in their intra-class competitions. Elite actors who have the support of the public—however such support is defined—acquire symbolic power to be used within the political realm to influence policy outcomes. The corollary of the public's capacity to enable elite actors is the capacity to constrain elite actors. Elections provide a clear example of this principle; as electoral victory represents a gain in symbolic power and objective political power, electoral loss signifies constraint. However, as there are multiple mechanisms through which the public can express its support, thus *granting* symbolic power, there are multiple corresponding mechanisms through which the public can *devalue* or *negate* the accrued symbolic power of elite actors. To the extent that the structures and institutions of contemporary democratic societies interpellate citizens not as self-directing agents, but rather as passive choice-makers (i.e. consumers), the validity of saying "no" becomes a fundamental assumption of the shared lifeworld. As such, the desire to constrain unacceptable elite behaviors extends into all modalities of individual existence where elite/non-elite dynamics exist.

The ability to say no, however, does not guarantee a corresponding response from elites; if this were the case, it would be possible to say that citizens truly control elite behavior. Instead, the ultimate point of attempts at elite constraint is to alter the strategic considerations of elite actors deployed within their competitive environment through threats to the accrued symbolic capital of elites (both individually and in groups).[14] The overall effectiveness of such attempts at elite constraint depends upon a variety of factors, not the least of which is that the mechanisms of elite constraint must be appropriately suited to the context of the elite action or event which precipitates a negative public reaction.

Public attempts to constrain elite actions or behaviors *must* contain an actual or perceived threat to the symbolic capital held by the transgressor of the public's sentiments (or a sufficiently large threat to the symbolic order at large) in order to potentially be successful. As strategic considerations, the specific means through which the public attempts to constrain elites must, as the saying goes, hit them where it hurts; the spectrum of such means may be grouped into four categories: physical, institutional, economic, and social. While these mechanisms of constraint will be examined separately, they are rarely utilized exclusively.

Physical Mechanisms

First and foremost, the public possesses a capacity to constrain elite behaviors through physical means. A wide variety of activities may be considered physical mechanisms of constraint, their shared defining characteristic being an objective manifestation of segments of the public that is presented before both the elite layer and other segments of the public in a conspicuous manner.

At the outset, it is worth noting that political violence, either in the form of a revolutionary movement, or in the form of discrete acts, would not properly represent attempts of constraint. Constraint is the public's means of partially influencing the symbolic order, or more specifically, the conditions under which the social powers of elite agents can be legitimately wielded. The existence of a field of dominance, as well as the general differentiation between those inside and outside of that field, are not *in themselves* challenged through acts of constraint. By contrast, political violence represents efforts to either replace one dominant group with another, or to establish a new social ordering based on a different principle of domination. Certainly, acts of political violence may be *motivated* by discontent with or outright rejection of the dominant symbolic ordering within their context;

however, as, under the Weberian definition, the legitimacy of the state's use of violence proportional to acts of political violence against it *cannot* be negated, political violence lies outside of the concept of constraint.

Through physical mechanisms of constraint, manifestations of symbolic power which serve to structure or order groups within society may be negated to the extent that they are incongruent with objective reality. Symbolic power, particularly as utilized within the realm of public issues, involves a kind of world-making power, according to Bourdieu. Elites struggle to structure the symbolic order by asserting the existence of groups, defining their characteristics, ideals, beliefs, oppositions, and determining their representation; directly relevant to electoral politics, elite political actors depict themselves as the embodiment of their various constituencies (e.g. Bob Smith is a *true* conservative). To the extent that elite actors possess sufficient symbolic capital, such perceptions of groups and identities are unchallenged and replicated throughout the larger social order in a generally unspoken manner.

Protests, marches, rallies, or other similar forms of political activity may serve as effective mechanisms of constraint by representing group attributes in a manner contrary to existing perceptions.[15] Public displays of solidarity or pride by marginalized groups convey a challenge to elite actors who, often dismissing these groups as being unorganized or of insignificant size, would continue to exclude them from the social and political order. Elite actors continuing to advocate marginalization or exclusion risk a loss of symbolic capital in the form of reputation, as the discrepancy with objective reality brings their judgment into question. By such means, segments of the public—especially disadvantaged or otherwise excluded segments—effectively place boundaries on the manner in which they are situated within the public and symbolic order; no amount of protest will ever *force* elite actors to recognize the legitimacy of a specific group or identity, but it may create a sufficiently high cost for the failure to do so.

The overall effectiveness, however, of such displays of group strength and solidarity, is itself limited by the lawful parameters of public behavior. Compliance with the lawful bounds of conduct necessarily imparts a degree of officialdom to the display; elite actors cannot challenge the validity of lawful public displays without necessarily devaluing their own accrued symbolic capital by discounting the symbolic power of the state itself. Elite actors within conventional political roles (e.g. elected officials) are thus highly sensitive to lawful forms of physical constraint, as such actions effectively leverage the symbolic power of the state against the elite layer.

Non-violent public displays outside of the lawful boundaries of conduct may still be effective in negating symbolic capital, but in a different manner. Unlawful, non-violent displays may be legitimately suppressed through the police powers of the state, so long as force is used in a proportional manner. Disproportionate use of force, however, is far more difficult to legitimize, and carries a persistent risk of appearing as blatant domination, as evidenced by historical examples such as the occupation of the Dharasana Salt

Works (India, 1930) and the June 4th Incident (China, 1989). By authorizing disproportionate use of force in reaction to unlawful, yet non-violent displays (e.g. acts of civil disobedience), elites effectively negate their own symbolic capital by breaking the pretense that something *other than* self-interest guides their use of state violence.

Institutional Mechanisms

Institutional mechanisms of constraint operate on a similar principle as physical mechanisms of constraint; the symbolic power of the state can be partially directed by the public through the various forms of institutional participation available. Elite actors *must* recognize the legitimacy of institutional participation in order to maintain any symbolic power derived from association with the state.

The most visible form of institutional constraint is the electoral process; as emphasized by the elite-realist approach, electoral losses provide a rough guide as to what the public will or will not find acceptable. However, given the multiplicity of issues involved in contemporary elections, inferences of the direct cause of an electoral loss may be very difficult. Clearer processes of elite action and public reaction may be seen through other institutional processes. Legal processes, for example, necessarily involve challenges to discrete actions of the state or individuals. The legal system may be a fairly versatile means of constraint, depending on the conditions under which lawsuits may be initiated; legal challenges, however, also involve higher stakes, as the winning party receives a nearly immutable grant of legal sanctification.

Economic Mechanisms

Economic mechanisms of constraint use market forces, rather than the state, as a means of setting boundaries of elite behavior. Sometimes referred to as "consumer activism," economic mechanisms of constraint are particularly useful in contexts where the elite actions in question originate outside of the political realm. Consistent with the "hit them where it hurts" principle, one component of economic mechanisms of constraint is a negation, or more realistically, a reduction, of the economic capital held by the offending elite actor or organization. When an economic entity, or representative thereof, violates the public's sentiments, the public may attempt to constrain it by refusing future business. As with electoral loss, however, the effects of such actions may not be directly attributable to public reactions, as flows of commerce are affected by any number of factors. What is more essential, therefore, for successful attempts at economic constraint (e.g. boycotts), is that the symbolic capital of the commercial entity is threatened as well; the actions of the offending actor or entity *must* be depicted as illegitimate in order to decouple the constraint attempt from regular market forces.

Successful depictions of illegitimacy, however, are not easily constructed. Claims of illegitimacy stemming from illegal actions are unlikely to threaten the symbolic power of commercial actors, as responses to such actions come from the state; firms committing illegal acts violate the public's interests as embodied in laws, not necessarily the public's trust. Similarly, bad business practices cannot be the grounds for claims of illegitimacy, as such practices will ultimately be resolved through regular market forces. Rather, claims of illegitimacy on moral or ethical grounds are most likely to negate the symbolic capital of a commercial actor, as such claims cannot be disposed of by other means.

The effectiveness of economic mechanisms of constraint thus depends upon a certain degree of visibility, as well as a clear and consistent "message" regarding the behavior of the commercial actor. Furthermore, this message must resonate with a sufficiently large pool of potential customers/clients to reach a critical mass of lost business. Even then, participation in economic constraint requires a level of flexibility in economic choices that not all members of the public may possess; among those that do have such flexibility, moral commitments and ethical standards do not always supplant individual economic interests. Economic mechanisms of constraint, while powerful in their capacity to set boundaries on actors beyond the reach of the political system, are thus limited by narrow conditions for success.

Social Mechanisms

A fourth and final category is comprised of social mechanisms of constraint, which are attempts to negate the symbolic capital held by elite actors within the realm of public communication. Unlike other mechanisms of constraint, social mechanisms do not require intermediating forces, such as elections or market forces, for their functioning; social constraint works by directly confronting the perceptions and reputations of elite actors. As such, social mechanisms of constraint are highly versatile, and may be utilized against elite actors of nearly all fields and possessing most any composition of capital.

Social mechanisms of constraint function by exploiting the nature of symbolic capital itself. As previously discussed, symbolic capital can be understood as reputation; elite actors are perceived as possessing certain qualities, commitments, or powers of judgment which convey a credit of validity to their actions or statements. Elite actors possessing symbolic capital are believed, followed, or trusted by the public, because they align with the public's perceptions of believability or trustworthiness; the content or significance of the actions of elite actors is *presumed* to be valid (i.e. consistent with the actor's stated goals, commitments, and previous actions) by their constituencies in the social whole.

Occupation of such a sacrosanct position within the political realm requires intense labor, especially for the maintenance of symbolic capital. According to Bourdieu:

> [I]t is because his specific capital is a pure fiduciary value which depends on representation, opinion, belief, fides, that the man of politics, like the man of honor, is especially vulnerable to suspicions, malicious misrepresentations and scandal, in short, to everything that threatens belief and trust, by bringing to light the hidden and secret acts and remarks of the present or the past which can undermine present acts and remarks and discredit their author... [Political capital] can be conserved only at the cost of unceasing work which is necessary both to accumulate credit and to avoid discredit: hence all the precautions, the silences, and the disguises, imposed on public personalities, who are forever forced to stand before the tribunal of public opinion, their constant need to ensure that they neither say nor do anything which might contradict their present or past professions of faith, or might show up their inconsistency over the course of time.[16]

Utilization of symbolic capital within the political realm thus requires a complex form of consistency of embodied representation. Consistency of statements or actions over time is only partially significant, as most any change can be rationally explained; rather, elite actors operating within the public realm must be consistent in their self-representation as a sincere and authentic representative of their constituent groups. Failure to maintain such consistency jeopardizes an actor's symbolic capital to the extent that it disrupts the structuring of the constituent group itself; inconsistent actions and statements by a political agent perceived as authentically embodying, for example, a "religious conservative" identity introduce ambiguities in the nature of "religious conservatism." Left uncorrected, such ambiguities throw into relief the manufactured nature of "religious conservatives" as a constituent group, and, in so doing, risk the creation of ripple effects within the whole of the symbolic order.

The overall stability of the symbolic order, however, is maintained by the structural characteristics of the elite realm. As the elite realm is inherently competitive, elite actors *will* labor to maintain the consistency of their self-representation in order to conserve their symbolic power. Should they make an insufficient effort to do so, competing elite actors will either make bids for the embodied leadership of the existing constituent group, or attempt to structure new constituent groups from its fragments. Furthermore, the elite realm is inherently *selective*, especially in regard to involvement in the political field. Commitment to what Bourdieu refers to as the "political game" of structuring and restructuring constituent groups and their representative identities is mandatory, making the political field partially collusive in nature; those failing to maintain the illusory nature of the political game risk ostracism, marginalization, and denigration not from the public, but from fellow elite actors.

Social constraint can thus be understood as the obligatory adherence to shared norms—both the norms of particular fields within the larger elite layer, as well as the norms of the constituent groups that an elite actor claims to represent. Under most circumstances, adherence to these sets of norms is automatically self-enforced by the structural characteristics of the elite layer. Individuals outside of the elite layer may, of course, make their own determinations of the reputations of elite actors; however, such individual determinations are unlikely to have a significant impact on elite behavior. Even if numerous others make similar determinations, such judgments will likely remain in seriality until catalyzed by the strategic interventions of a competing elite actor.

The seeming inability of the public to affect the distribution of symbolic capital *in a spontaneous or autonomous manner* echoes the assessment of public passivity from the elite-realist and elite-liberal approaches. According to Bourdieu, however, this is not necessarily a function of passivity; the crafting of a cohesive group and narration of its shared identity and interests is an intense labor which requires cultural and social capital. Such skills in symbolic production are concentrated in the dominant class, and not readily available to those outside it. As such, groups in society (especially in the form of classes) exist because their elite representatives assert that they do:

> The "working class" exists in and through the body of representatives who give it an audible voice and a visible presence, and in and through the belief in its existence which this body of plenipotentiaries succeeds in imposing, by its mere existence and its representations, on the basis of affinities which objectively unite the members of the same "class on paper" as a probable group.[17]

The use of social constraint as an independent check on elite actions and behaviors thus appears contradictory: to the extent that groups or segments in the social whole possess a set of sensibilities or interests that can be offended by elite actions, to the extent that the public possesses "boundaries" which trigger its reactivity, such sensibilities, interests, and boundaries are partially structured by members of the dominant class themselves.

The Practicability of Constraint

Mechanisms of constraint represent attempts to negate (or at least devalue) the symbolic capital of an elite actor, group, or institution that has gone outside of the boundaries of what is considered acceptable by segments of the non-elite population. As previously mentioned, mechanisms of constraint are rarely used in an exclusive manner; rather, most historical examples of successful efforts at social change involve combinations of mechanisms of constraint. For example, the Civil Rights Movement (United States, 1954–68) included a variety of efforts using all mechanisms of constraint: the Montgomery Bus Boycott combined an economic mechanism of constraint with the physical presence of carpools and "freedom walkers," the use of lawsuits by the NAACP Legal Defense Fund represented institutional mechanisms of constraint, etc.

The consideration of which combinations of mechanisms may be used in attempts to constrain offending elites is structured by a variety of factors, not the least of which is the *source* of the public grievance, particularly, the nature of the symbolic capital that the constraint effort seeks to negate. Considerations of source, however, only serve to partially structure constraint efforts, primarily through the elimination of non-applicable mechanisms. For example, institutional mechanisms of constraint only work in contexts where the offending elite actor(s) are within the reach of institutional processes (e.g. elections, legal proceedings); similarly, economic mechanisms are only really applicable when the elite actor or institution's standing in a competitive market is at stake.

What is arguably more important is the *practicability* of certain mechanisms of constraint, which can be understood as a range of dispositions towards constraint efforts that emerges from the structural contexts and perceived costs or risks associated with the usage of mechanisms of constraint. Practicability thus emerges from the public's considerations of what *can be done*, what is *acceptable to do*, and what is *worth the risk of doing*.

The practicability of various forms of constraint within a given polity is determined in part by that polity's structural-institutional characteristics. The various institutional rights which characterize liberal democratic polities (e.g. rights of peaceable assembly, rights of speech and expression, rights of association) enable the practicability of physical, institutional, and social mechanisms of constraint. The presence of such rights, however, is not an absolute prerequisite, as the histories of authoritarian and transitioning states are rife with protest movements. Rather, the lack of institutional political rights may encourage protest; in contexts where institutional mechanisms of constraint are not available, aggrieved segments of the public may have an increased disposition towards the usage of physical mechanisms.

The practicability of constraint is also determined in part by the perceptions of the acceptability and usefulness of constraint efforts; such subjective (i.e. cultural) factors, however, are themselves structured to no small degree by the internal dynamics of the elite realm. In this regard, various statements or policy actions may be understood as efforts to reduce the practicability and/or effectiveness of mechanisms of constraint, without necessarily prohibiting them. Through various means, elite actors may attempt to *insulate* themselves from negative public reactions by making certain constraint efforts riskier or more difficult. Such efforts at insularity (which will be explored in greater depth in Chapter 4) are not oriented at increasing individual stores of symbolic capital, but rather at preserving the larger symbolic order by negating the public's capacity to negate symbolic power.

Conclusion

As derived from Bourdieu's sociological concepts, competition within the elite layers of societies involves actors and institutions from a variety of fields, each possessing different quantities and compositions of capital (i.e.

different kinds of social power). Elite competition involves struggles both for leadership *within* their fields and for dominance *across* fields, with the realm of public decision making (i.e. politics) representing a shared competitive arena. Political competition, however, requires some degree of public involvement, creating a variety of opportunities for individuals *outside* of the elite realm to partially structure the actions and behaviors of elites; such opportunities take the form of mechanisms of constraint. As will be examined in the following chapters, new practices within networked communication suggest an increased capacity of individuals outside of the elite realm to participate in the symbolic production of group identities, and thus to exercise their capacity for social constraint in a more autonomous manner.

Notes

1 Bourdieu, *The Logic of Practice*, 118.
2 Bourdieu, "The Forms of Capital," 15.
3 Bourdieu, *The Logic of Practice*, 192.
4 Bourdieu, "Social Space and Symbolic Power," 23.
5 Bourdieu, *Language and Symbolic Power*, 230–1.
6 Wacquant, "From ruling class to field of power," 22.
7 Ibid., 26.
8 At various points, Bourdieu refers to this power of the state as symbolic violence. However, such terminology implies negation of aspects of the symbolic order; manipulation appears to be a preferable alternative, as it implies both negation and legitimization (i.e. the granting of legitimacy).
9 Bourdieu, *Language and Symbolic Power*, 181.
10 Rubin and Drucker, "Romney's 13.9% Tax Rate Spotlights Wealthy Investors' Breaks."
11 "Republican Debate Transcript, Tampa, Florida, January 2012."
12 "Obergefell v. Hodges 576 U.S. ___ (2015)."
13 Ibid.
14 It is important to note at this point, that through attempting to constrain elite behavior, the public is not necessarily attempting to acquire symbolic capital for itself, but rather to chip away at the artifice of elites, and in so doing, partially structure the elite realm from the outside.
15 Bourdieu, "Social Space and Symbolic Power," 20.
16 Bourdieu, *Language and Symbolic Power*, 192–3.
17 Ibid., 251.

Bibliography

Bourdieu, Pierre. *Language and Symbolic Power*. Cambridge: Polity Press, 1991.
Bourdieu, Pierre. *The Logic of Practice*. Stanford, CA: Stanford University Press, 1990.
Bourdieu, Pierre. "Social Space and Symbolic Power." *Sociological Theory* 7, no. 1 (1989): 14–25.
Bourdieu, Pierre. "The Forms of Capital." In *Handbook of Theory and Research for the Sociology of Education*, 241–258. New York: Greenwood Press, 1986.

50 A Theory of Constrained Elitism

"Obergefell v. Hodges 576 U.S. ___ (2015)." *Justia Law*. Accessed August 16, 2015. https://supreme.justia.com/cases/federal/us/576/14-556/.

"Republican Debate Transcript, Tampa, Florida, January 2012." Council on Foreign Relations. Accessed August 11, 2015. www.cfr.org/elections/republican-debate-transcript-tampa-florida-january-2012/p27180.

Rubin, Richard, and Jesse Drucker. "Romney's 13.9% Tax Rate Spotlights Wealthy Investors' Breaks." *Bloomberg Business*, January 25, 2012. www.bloomberg.com/news/articles/2012-01-24/romney-paid-13-9-percent-tax-rate-on-21-6-million-2010-income.

Wacquant, Loïc JD. "From ruling class to field of power: An interview with Pierre Bourdieu on La Noblesse d'Etat." *Theory, Culture and Society* 10, no. 3 (1993): 19–44.

3 The Contemporary Networked Public Sphere

> *Using computerized lists and on-line networks for different interest groups, individual citizens will be able to send their own promotional material, propaganda, and publicity of all kinds in all formats to individuals, groups, and political representatives of their own choosing. There will be a continuing flow of audio, video, and written communications, dialogue exchanges, yes/no votes and polls, position papers and programs, interviews, speeches, presentations, and advertisements—all rattling around in cyberspace and all instantly available on command.*[1]
>
> Lawrence Grossman, *The Electronic Republic*

Introduction

While networked communications have not created a system of electronic direct democracy in the United States, as foreseen by early internet advocates such as Grossman (former president of PBS and NBC News), the vision of enhanced individual participation and production within an intense circulation of information streams seems to have fully materialized. Within the realm of contemporary public communication, individual choice of information sources has greatly expanded, as has the capacity of individuals to create and distribute information independently of government or market structures.

Within mass-mediated communicative relationships, subject positions are relatively static: those in the audience function as consumers with little to no interaction with those who produce communicative content (e.g. members of the media system).[2] Networked communication processes, on the other hand, rely upon open and dynamic relationships and organization of production; according to Benkler:

> [T]he networked environment makes possible a new modality of organizing production: radically decentralized, collaborative, and nonproprietary; based on sharing resources and outputs among widely distributed, loosely connected individuals who cooperate with each other without relying on either market signals or managerial commands.[3]

Such flexibility—for organization, processes, and relationships—underlies all aspects of network society, according to Castells.[4] Specific to networked communication, this flexibility suggests a transcendence of both the fixity and homogeneity associated with mass subjectivity; within the networked environment, individuals outside of the media system possess substantially more capacity to produce and distribute information than within the mass-mediated environment.

The expanded communicative marketplace enabled by networked communications encompasses a variety of forms of production. The changed marketplace (i.e. patterns and relationships of production and consumption) for cultural goods is frequently cited as an example of the anti-hierarchical potential of networked communications. In relation to cultural goods, the openness of the communicative marketplace is evidenced in the alteration and reappropriation of cultural works (e.g. music and films); this is not simply a manner of changing the internal composition of the institutions of cultural goods production, but of altering the relationships between producers and consumers. As Mark Poster writes:

> The consumer can now be a producer, reproducer, distributor, and creator of cultural objects. Thereby digital technology undermines the systems of controls that were associated with fixed cultural objects and brings control of culture itself into question by opening cultural objects to an unlimited process of alterations.[5]

Networked communications technologies thus offer increased communicative agency for individuals within the realm of cultural goods production.

Specific to politics, communicative agency within the networked public sphere manifests itself as public communication—the dissemination and discussion of information and arguments regarding issues of collective concern. Networked communications may thus be utilized by individuals to become informed about public issues and to organize various forms of political participation, rather than to form alternative structures for political decision-making (i.e. e-democracy). Communication in the networked public is thus not oriented towards *replacing* institutional structures of representative democracy, but rather towards *enhancing* them by creating a more robust public—one with a greater capacity to understand the decisions of representatives and the actions of the political system while simultaneously avoiding being subject to demagoguery and elite manipulation.

Such a vision of a robust, informed citizenry acting as the guarantor of honest government echoes Jefferson's exhortations on the functional necessity of a free press for the representative system. A free press, according to Jefferson, ensures that public opinion remains in constant flux, thus preventing the public from becoming overly docile; public opinion represents a well of potential energy which "must be submitted to" by political leaders.[6] As a conduit for uninhibited flows of information, the press provides the raw material needed for individuals within the public to utilize their good judgment and common sense. From a 1787 letter to Carrington, Jefferson writes:

> I am persuaded myself that the good sense of the people will always be found to be the best army. They may be led astray for a moment, but will soon correct themselves. The people are the only censors of their governors: and even their errors will tend to keep these to the true principles of their institution... The way to prevent these irregular interpositions of the people is to give them full information of their affairs thro' the channel of the public papers, & to contrive that those papers should penetrate the whole mass of the people.[7]

The indirect relevance for Jeffersonian thought is underscored by his distrust of the press. In his second inaugural address, Jefferson directly identifies the judgment and indignation of the public as the natural correctives for the press's potential "demoralizing licentiousness."[8] As will be discussed later in this chapter, new practices of networked communication, specifically, new media applications (i.e. blogs), may attempt to hold the press accountable to the public; rather than rely upon professional ethics or governmental regulations, increased competition between traditional and new forms of media may serve as an effective guarantor of quality information.

Grossman's vision thus resembles what Siebert refers to as a libertarian theory of the press. According to Siebert, in the libertarian theory the responsibility to make determinations regarding public interest lies with the public itself, rather than with journalists; the libertarian theory of the press advises to:

> let the public at large be subjected to a barrage of information and opinion, some of it possibly true, some of it possibly false, and some of it containing elements of both. Ultimately, the public could be trusted to digest the whole, to discard that not in the public interest and to accept that which served the needs of the individual and of the society of which he is a part.[9]

Such a vision of public interest emerging from within the public itself through the actions of an active reading public within a diverse information context is highly consistent with Glenn Reynolds' assessment that "the press" and "the media" cease to be external to the public under networked communications. Instead of depending upon professional journalism, Reynolds' regrettably named construct of "we-dia" exists as a communal and peer-based effort of production, distribution, and critique of information.[10]

To the extent that such positive depictions of networked communication are correct, the transition from mass-mediated to networked forms of communication would seem to be highly significant for the larger question of elite/non-elite relations and the manipulation of symbolic power. Before re-considering these issues, however, further examination of the changes in the structures of contemporary communication is necessary.

Mediated and Networked Structures

Discussions of the public sphere are frequently comparative in nature, juxtaposing communicative practices before and after the widespread availability of internet communication; however, across scholarly and popular literature, there are few consistently applied comparative methodologies. One popular method is based upon the distinction between "new media" (i.e. those media applications based on internet communications technologies) and "old" or "legacy" media (i.e. existing media technologies, such as radio and print). While this comparison of underlying technology may be useful in terms of the business models of media firms, it has only minimal application to analyses of social relationships engendered by communications technologies. Furthermore, the distinction itself is increasingly problematic as legacy media firms increasingly utilize new media platforms for their content distribution.[11]

Relevant to political economy studies of communication, Yochai Benkler utilizes a distinction between social production and firm-based production; under social production, intellectual properties, information, and cultural goods are developed voluntarily by peers within a networked environment, where firm-based production occurs in the context of contractual labor and hierarchical management of production processes. In the more specific context of public communication, the domination of firm-based production by mass media institutions constitutes a mass-mediated public sphere, while new forms of social production of news and information indicate the emergence of a networked public sphere.[12]

This distinction between networked and mass-mediated public spheres is particularly useful for understanding the production and distribution of information. Within the contemporary United States, mass-mediated communications processes occur predominantly within commercial media markets; production occurs within hierarchically organized media firms and is oriented by the maximization of audience and the minimization of production cost. Networked communications, by contrast, provide a greater fluidity of subject positions within the production-distribution-consumption cycle of information and cultural goods. Simply stated, the information and cultural goods marketplace enabled by networked communication has little to no barriers to entry or costs of exit. Furthermore, the scalable and relatively inexpensive nature of storing digitized information allows a vast plurality of information streams to exist simultaneously and indefinitely.

The Culture of the Networked Public

The communications environment and marketplace under networked communications is thus significantly different from that under mass-mediated communications, especially in regard to productive capacity of individuals outside of conventional channels of mediated communication. Such structural changes entail both an increase in the productive capacity of the public and a broader cultural shift regarding the meaning of being "the consumer" in contemporary capitalism. In *Remix*, Lawrence Lessig offers an analysis of protection of intellectual property from both a cultural and legal perspective. According to Lessig, strict copyright laws and business models oriented only towards individual consumption risk locking American society into a Read/Only (RO) culture. In such a culture, folk experimentation and amateur creativity are sacrificed for consistent and widespread distribution of cultural goods. By contrast, Read/Write (RW) culture views recreation and recontextualization as part of the process of cultural distribution; culture goods attain their full significance through being shared, rather than simply distributed. Similarly, by inviting the public to contribute or otherwise respond, RW culture "asks something more of the audience," and may serve to replicate of norms of reciprocity and mutual listening.[13]

While Lessig discusses RW culture as being rooted in the amateur performance of cultural goods (e.g. singing in the streets), there is an obvious connection to communicative practices within the networked public. Individuals "re-write" information streams at three levels. The first level is the text (or content) of a particular piece of information; the ideal example of such re-writing is individual commenting (on blog posts, YouTube videos, etc.). On the second level, individuals can directly affect the distribution and organization of information streams by adding descriptive metadata to a particular piece of information or through social bookmarking tools designed to signify to other information seekers that a particular item is worth reading. On a final layer, individuals indirectly affect the organization of information streams, as their online habits and choices are aggregated and analyzed as measures of significance.[14] Survey research on social network users in the United States suggests such practices of participatory news consumption are fairly common; in a 2014 study by the Pew Research Center, fifty percent of social network users reported sharing or reposting news articles, with slightly less than half of users also commenting on or discussing news stories online.[15]

While production and flows of information are becoming increasingly networked within the public sphere, the structures of the mass-mediated public sphere continue to exist and show few indications of going away; existing institutions of mass mediation (i.e. those of the commercial media system) still hold considerable steering power, but in less of a monopolized form. Similarly, while new practices of communication may empower the public in various ways, they do not eliminate the complex relationships and interdependencies between media and economic institutions within the public sphere. The functional capacity of the contemporary public sphere to act as a conduit for articulating collective problems, formulating public opinion, and holding political and economic power holders accountable is increasing, but nonetheless constrained by existing structures of communicative, economic, and political power.

The contemporary public sphere, therefore, is perhaps best understood as existing in both mass-mediated and networked states—a kind of superposition, wherein the relationships and processes of both states are still evident. Institutionalized media firms still dominate the realm of cultural production, and the overall forces of symbolic production are concentrated within the elite layer; those outside the elite layer are increasingly capable of symbolic and cultural production, but are not capable of displacing existing elite actors and institutions. Within this superposition, the relationships between existing communicative positions and spaces (i.e. information consumer/producer), as well as the processes and capacities of communicative production, become more complex, making a new conceptual "map" of the public sphere necessary.

Segmentation and Stratification in the Public Sphere

Despite the gradual expansion of political egalitarianism within liberal democracies throughout history, public spheres are fundamentally unequal systems. The internal dynamics of the public sphere, especially those related to its stratified nature, have been carefully developed throughout the works of German sociologist Bernhard Peters. Inequality in the contemporary public sphere should not be understood as a function of exclusion (i.e. limited application of civil rights and liberties), but rather in terms of "graduated asymmetries" in the capacities to communicate within the public sphere. Some asymmetries occur naturally, as individuals possess different levels of political sophistication, cultural capital, and general interest in public issues. Most asymmetry, however, occurs as the result of practical divisions of labor within complex societies; certain positions—pastors, journalists, elected officials, etc.—necessarily entail a greater capacity to "be heard" than other positions.[16]

This type of "functional" differentiation is fairly straightforward within mass-mediated communications—speaker positions have a structural capacity for communicative activities, while audience positions do not. However, as previously discussed, the "speaker" and "audience" subject positions inherited from mass-mediated relationships seem insufficient within contemporary public communication, particularly in regard to their functional differences. Rather, to make sense of stratified positions in the networked public sphere, it may be useful to first consider a range of *actual communicative-productive activities*. With this in mind, multiple levels of productive activity can be conceptualized, encompassing the expanded range of communicative practices in the networked public sphere and providing a basis for differentiating between multiple stratified positions.

At the highest end of the range shown in Table 3.1 is *elite production*. Communicative activities at this level roughly correspond to those of the functional positions of "speakers" within mass-mediated relationships. Information streams produced at this level are distributed via the most prominent distribution channels (e.g. national media outlets) or via the most prestigious channels and organizations of more specialized publics (i.e. *The Journal of the American Medical Association*). Communicative activities at this level are highly visible, and are oriented towards wide audiences of national or international scales. Understandably, only a very small percentage of communicative activities occur at this level.[17]

By contrast, at the lowest end of the spectrum of productive activity is *consumption*—effectively the lack of production. Roughly corresponding to the category of "audience" within mass-mediated relationships, communicative activities at this level involve the passive reception of information streams by individuals. To the extent that patterns of consumption can be monitored and/or quantified (e.g. television ratings), some forms of feedback can be indirectly extracted as a by-product of consumption; however as they do not necessarily entail willful communicative action on behalf of the consumer, such forms of feedback should not be considered productive activities.

The continued existence of these categories of communicative activity suggests that practices of networked communication or "new media" have not eliminated audience and speaker positions, but instead have created a fairly vast range of activities in between them. This middle range can be divided, yielding two additional categories of communicative-productive activities: *intermediate production* and *active consumption*.

The communicative-productive activity of *active consumption* combines the consumption of information streams with a willfully created feedback component. A wide and diverse body of contemporary practices fall within this

Table 3.1 Levels of Production in the Networked Public

Level	Mechanism	Characteristics
Elite production	Mass media outlets, leading national outlets	High visibility; directed at broadest possible audience
Intermediate production	Blogs, social media, discussion boards	Limited visibility; specialized or niche audience
Active consumption	Commenting, social bookmarking	Dependent upon structural "invitation"
Passive consumption	Market research	Quantification of consumer behavior

category: writing product reviews for purchases from online retailers, providing feedback ratings from online auction transactions, commenting on blog posts or online news articles, adding links to social bookmarking sites, etc. It is important to note that practices of active consumption do not involve the creation of new information streams, but rather the voluntary addition of content to existing information streams. Active consumption is thus dependent upon the structural "invitation" for users to add content; simply stated, websites have to be designed in a manner which invites feedback or comments. While content generated through active consumption may authentically represent "voices" in the public, it is inherently constrained by the deliberate choices of the designers of online fora; as such, the risk of the structural exclusion of minority or unpopular voices limits the overall significance of active consumption. Furthermore, the willful decision by individuals to participate in acts of active consumption requires recognition of information consumption as a social practice, or what Lessig refers to as a "read/write" cultural disposition. Without such a disposition—either as a function of individual characteristics, or socio-cultural norms—structural opportunities for active consumption ultimately go unfulfilled.

Of far greater significance is the production of new information streams at the non-elite level. Either as the result of deliberate individual or collaborative efforts (e.g. blog publishing) or emerging from collective communication (e.g. message boards), such *intermediate production* constitutes the great bulk of communicative activity within the networked public. Information streams produced at this intermediate level represent the outputs of sites/blogs in the "long tail" of power law distributions as well as the nearly infinite niches which fail to garner mass attention. A common (and overused) term to signify such a realm of communicative activity within the networked environment is "the blogosphere."[18]

Stratification in the Networked Public

Conceptualizing stratification in terms of communicative-productive activities rather than functional position is not simply a change of terminology. Under mass-mediated communications, the number of real and putative elites—those with a potential to possess influence within the public sphere—is relatively small and easily linked to the "speaker" category; elite and non-elite status are effectively nested within speaker and audience positions. However, due to the lowered (if not eliminated) barriers to entry into the general "market" of public communication brought about by networked communications technologies, the number of "speakers" before the public has increased along with the ranks of the actors attempting to compete at the elite level. Simultaneously, as elite status is decoupled from "speaker" functionality, the distinctions between "speaker" and "audience" as subject positions become subject to more gradation. Thus, a new typology of status positions within the realm of public communication appears necessary.

The contemporary public sphere can be conceptualized as consisting of three main strata or levels, the highest of which is the *public elite*. This level is comprised of the actors and institutions of national opinion leadership, as well as those actors and institutions mobilized in the process of information production. The variety of public actors which Peters (and Habermas) identifies as speakers within the public sphere—journalists, experts, advocates for issue/interest groups, representatives of civic organizations, party leadership—exist at this elite level. Communicative actions produced at the elite level are oriented towards large portions of the public at its highest meaningful abstraction (e.g. at the national level), although actors within lower strata of the public elite may necessarily orient themselves towards more limited audiences.

Claiming the existence of an elite stratum within the public sphere is neither controversial nor innovative; equally non-controversial is the observation of the existence of a *general public*, whose primary function (within mass-mediated relationships) is to act as the audience—the public to whom the public elite address themselves. The distinction (and relationship) between the public elite and the general public retains relevance to the extent that mass-mediated communications retain their relevance; what I suggest, is that the elite-public axis fails to adequately account for practices and relationships of networked communications and that the various forms of intermediate production facilitated by networked communication cannot be properly contextualized within the general public, as so few members of the public actually become involved in this form of production. This skewed distribution of the various forms of non-elite production is captured by the popular 90–9–1 rule-of-thumb, which holds that for any one-hundred internet users, ninety simply consume content, nine undertake forms of active consumption, and only one engages in intermediate production.[19] To account for the various activities and processes that seem to fall outside of the elite-public axis, a third level—an *intermediate public*—must be introduced and theorized as distinct from both the public elite and the general public.

At its most basic conceptualization, the intermediate public is the space of communicative activity which does not correspond to either pattern of elite information production or relatively passive consumption by the general public. Individuals within this intermediate space act on their capacity to engage in communicative production (unlike individuals within the general public), yet do not possess a sufficient volume of influence or power within the public sphere to truly compete with elite actors. This, however, is only a partial explanation; a more thorough distinction is necessary to fully illustrate the differences in the respective practical logics of the public sphere at each of its different levels. Before drilling into each level, a brief sketch of the relationships between the various levels may be helpful. Figure 3.1 offers a brief sketch of the types of relationships between the public elite, the intermediate public, and the general public.

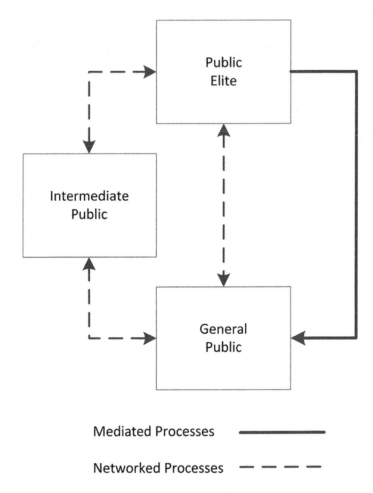

Figure 3.1 Mediated and Networked Relationships

At the level of the public elite, as previously mentioned, communicative action is oriented towards a maximal audience for either the acquisition of or exercise of influence. As the elite are best defined via their (mediated) relationship with the general public, and the general public represents the largest and least demanding audience, communicative action by the public elite is primarily oriented towards the general public. In the competition for influence, however, various strategic advantages can be achieved via intermediate level processes, thus no small portion of elite production is oriented towards the intermediate public.

The general public receives inputs from both the public elite and the intermediate public; given the high degree of interrelation of various forms of media, differentiation between input *types* provides little useful information.[20] Input *paths*, however, may be insightful to the extent that they structure differing levels of production by the general public. Inviting active consumption has become de rigueur for information streams delivered via networked paths, and is increasingly practiced in mass-mediated paths as well (e.g. television news' solicitations of user feedback via email). Perhaps more significant, however, is the degree to which productions emanating from the intermediate public invite further intermediate production. Intermediate production occurs in the intermediate public; communicative actions emerging from the intermediate public do not simply represent sophisticated forms of feedback, but rather attempts of individuals to become constituent components of the public communication process. In the following sections, the internal dynamics and processes of each level will be examined in more depth.

The Struggle for Influence in the Networked Public

When viewed in its entirety, the public sphere (as modeled in levels of communicative activity in Figure 3.1) appears to be both an elitist and pluralist system. On the one hand, a limited stratum of elite public actors exists, whose actions guide, if not dominate, most public discourse; the vast majority of the public (i.e. the non-elite) engage in little to no communicative activity. On the other hand, this elite stratum is *internally* segmented and differentiated, with elite public actors emerging from a variety of contexts. Furthermore, communicative activities emerging from the intermediate public (as well as the institutions of civil society) create a seemingly endless stream of challenges and critiques of statements and actions of existing elite public actors, while simultaneously providing a potential springboard for putative elite actors. Thus, the public elite level of the public sphere is best understood as being an internally dynamic and competitive arena in which actors vie for the public's attention.[21] Consistent with the multipolar approach to elite competition discussed in previous chapters, competition at this elite level of the public sphere primarily involves the struggle between actors for symbolic capital in various forms.

Specific to the realm of public communication, elite public actors seek to *possess* influence by being recognized by the public as *being* influential.[22] As a function both of natural talents and previous competitive behaviors, some actors and institutions have a greater capacity to affect public opinions than others; the elite realm possesses a near monopoly over this form of symbolic power, yet its distribution *within* the elite realm is highly uneven. For purposes of understanding this distribution of public influence, Bernhard Peters' concepts regarding stratification in the public sphere are extremely useful. According to Peters, distributions of influence within the public sphere are a function of three main factors: authority, visibility, and network position.

The first factor involved in the formulation of public influence is authority, which can be provisionally defined as being recognized as competent or credible within the public sphere. According to Peters, authority contains both a pretense of epistemic or evaluative superiority and entails an expectation of deference of judgment on behalf of the non-authority:

> Public authority (or prestige) can refer to different forms of competence or credibility which are attributed to a person: empirical knowledge and cognitive ability, abilities of moral understanding and judgment or of evaluative judgment, impartiality, experience with particular problems, demonstrated analytical capacity, ability to propose solutions. Having authority gives credit to one's utterances, an advance of credibility, the expectation that one's judgments are true or appropriate.[23]

Authority can be increased or strengthened in two ways. First, by previous statements; individuals who have previously made meaningful contributions to public discourse are more likely, but not guaranteed, to be seen as authorities. Second, by institutional location; individual speakers gain authority when they are associated with prestigious institutions, communicative entities, or positions within the political system.

The second main component of influence in the public sphere is prominence or visibility. Simply stated, visibility is public attention, which is acquired primarily through functional roles or through social status. While visibility is a fairly straightforward concept, according to Peters, it is important that an actor's visibility is understood in proportion to the scope of the public in which s/he acquired it: speakers who are well known in limited publics (e.g. foreign policy circles, sociologists) are not likely to be well known by the general public.

At this point, the interactive nature of these two factors is likely apparent; authority and visibility are highly interconnected, yet one does not entail the other. For example, celebrities possess a great deal of visibility, but are not necessarily considered to be reliable sources of political judgment or analysis. Likewise, scientists who may possess expertise relevant to policy discourses are likely to lack visibility outside of their respective academic discipline. Clearly, for actors within the public sphere to have their voices heard, both authority and visibility are needed; the complementary nature of these factors is suggested by Peters' assertion that influence is "a multiplicative function of visibility and authority."

A final component of influence which Peters addresses is network positioning. Given that multiple nested hierarchies exist in the public sphere, actors can have a good deal of influence by virtue of being positioned favorably in relation to other influential actors without necessarily having visibility or authority. Peters writes:

> Being prominent and having a high reputation are the best conditions for seeing one's ideas distributed and accepted. But this is not in itself sufficient. Influence is also determined by institutional location and

relevant social connections. Journalists in certain positions, for instance, might not be especially well known personally, they might not necessarily have very high prestige (among the attentive public or the elite), but they might nevertheless have some influence because of their ability to get their ideas published in influential places.[24]

Such network positioning, according to Peters, may manifest itself as "behind-the-scenes" influence whereby actors "affect the circulation of ideas without directly contributing to them."

Within the public elite layer of the public sphere, the stratified nature of influence necessarily creates a form of competition between public actors for relative position in the public's eye. In an ideal "marketplace of ideas," such competition would likely be beneficial to the quality of public discourse in the long term; however, various characteristics of influence—as identified in the previous section—instead prompt elite public actors to choose dramatized presentation of issues over discursive presentations, and/or attempt to assert "moral authority" in regard to more controversial issues.[25] In particular, the nature of authority, as mediated through public communication, makes appeals to the public's rationality, a losing strategy within the competition for influence.

Authority within the public sphere is ultimately a matter of deference. At some point, individual members of the public adopt the arguments put forth by elite public actors and decide to cease any independent, active consideration of an issue. For such a grant of deference to occur, putative elite public actors must first make a sufficiently convincing *claim* of authority. Given the multiple connotations of the term "authority," a brief examination may be useful. In one usage, authority is something to be obeyed; law enforcement, parents, elected officials—to some degree, all are linked to a process of issuing commands with an expectation of compliance, lest some form of coercion be used. On the other hand, authority is something to be willingly believed; doctors, priests, experts—often, individuals voluntarily defer their judgment on specific issues to such authority figures. These distinctions, among many others, map "authority" into two distinct meanings: in-authority and an-authority. The distinction between in-authority and an-authority is based on the nature of the authority claim, and effectively represents positions with (separate) asymmetrical relationships between authority and non-authority. Authority is thus a separate category of social existence (in opposition to non-authority) wherein a distinct set of rules regarding justification for claims, statements, or demands applies.

In-authority can be provisionally defined as the characteristic of being *in a position* which conveys authority; this general category of authority is marked by an expectation that the authority figure will be obeyed, either out of obligation or fear of sanction. Examples of in-authority are fairly straightforward: police, judges, etc.

Separate from in-authority is an-authority; this form of authority is the characteristic of being viewed as being in possession of knowledge, skills, or expertise above and beyond that of the average person. While the in-authority carries an expectation of obedience, the an-authority carries an expectation of belief; where the in-authority conditions the actions of non-authorities, the an-authority conditions the beliefs and interpretations of facticity of non-authorities.[26] Examples of an-authorities are a bit more varied, as anyone who puts forth a claim of an authoritative knowledge or statement can be seen as a putative authority; not surprisingly, putative public actors (e.g. op-ed writers, pundits, cable news show hosts) fall under the category of an-authority.

Within the competition for influence at the public elite level, actors must "prove themselves" in some manner, by having their claims of authority status validated by the public. Such validation is essential, according to Flathman, as future statements of valid authorities attain a kind of privileged position of being subjected to less scrutiny. The ability of the public to make such judgments of validity, however, is problematic, as the granting of authority involves an epistemic gap between the public and the elite actor. Elite public actors must demonstrably possess some kind of knowledge, information, or perspective that is not readily available to the public; to the extent that some information is commonly known (or knowable), the public will have no reason to defer to the putative authority holder.[27] This epistemic gap, however, makes individuals in the public less than ideally suited to judge the authority claims of putative public actors, making some means through which the non-authority can overcome the epistemic gap and render judgments of authority claims necessary.

Statements and claims made in the context of an-authority are thus declaratory in nature, rather than based on rationality. The authority of any elite public actor is a function of the public's belief in the authority, not necessarily of the actors' demonstrated skills and abilities. To the extent that authority operates in this manner, elite public actors may gain a strategic advantage through portraying themselves as the embodiment of the qualities that make a person "believable" for a particular constituent audience. Competition for influence is therefore manifest through elite public actors attempting to position themselves vis-à-vis each other as the *de facto* authority for specific issue positions. The public sphere, according to Peters, is thus a realm of "controversy and discord," rather than rational or discursive processes. Elite competition

> is not only about a competition for public attention; it is also a matter of competition for the intellectual and moral leadership in their own camp that places a premium on intransigence and the demonstration of particular sensibilities.[28]

This emphasis on dramatization and competition makes the potential for resolution of public issues via consensus highly improbable. When contentious public issues actually do become stabilized over time, it is most likely the result of attrition. As specific issue positions lose their resonance within the general public, and thus cease to be attention generating, they are strategically abandoned by elite public actors.

The Political Economy of Media in the Networked Public

An additional consideration in regard to influence within the public sphere is the role of economic power. Some degree of visibility, as a component of influence, may be "purchased" by individual actors through various mechanisms of public relations and advertisement; to the extent, however, that an actor's visibility appears artificial, their authority is likely to correspondingly decrease. The naked usage of economic power to force specific opinions before the public will appear as domination, rather than deference.

Instead, economic capital may serve to structure communication in the public sphere by selectively *excluding* certain viewpoints from being fully articulated. Numerous contemporary media scholars argue that the dominance of commercial media firms (especially in the United States) serves to skew the content of information presented to the public through commercial biases. At its most basic level, commercial bias exists as a privileging of commercialized content over other forms of content, which is most noticeable as the deluge of advertising and product placement within contemporary media content. Specific to the framing of news stories, commercial bias manifests as a form of class bias wherein the voices of elite actors are prioritized. Robert McChesney cites coverage of various economic recovery initiatives under the Bush and Obama administrations as an example of such bias: while the bailout and restructuring of General Motors—which would directly affect hundreds of thousands of blue-collar workers—received relatively little attention, initiatives directed at stabilizing investment firms have been given ample coverage. According to McChesney, "Poor and working-class people are, for all intents and purposes, only newsworthy to the extent they get in the way of rich people."[29]

Commercial bias is perhaps more pernicious as the de facto elimination of non-capitalist ideals. This tendency—which Douglas Kellner has termed the "logic of exclusion"—limits the diversity of viewpoints made available through the major media channels. Kellner describes the "logic of exclusion" as such:

> Television's logic of accumulation dictates a logic of exclusion that condemns to silence those voices whose criticisms of the capitalist mode of production go beyond the boundaries allowed by the lords of the media ... The opinion spectrum that dominates television thus includes only those liberals and conservatives who tacitly agree that all discourse must take place within the framework of the existing system of

production and representative democracy, from which more radical views are rigorously excluded.[30]

This "logic of exclusion" dictates that the range of acceptable viewpoints regarding economics is thus limited to a fairly narrow choice between Clintonian neo-liberalism on the left and laissez-faire on the right. Edward Herman's research on public opinion and media utilizes media framing of global trade agreements and organizations (e.g. NAFTA, GATT, and the WTO) as a case study in commercial bias. According to Herman, coverage of the development of NAFTA generally ignored public sentiment against the trade agreement, and failed to adequately discuss the potential ramifications for labor and unskilled workers in the United States. Rather, free trade was presented as a natural extension of market freedom, the expansion of which would be beneficial to all parties involved.[31]

In addition to such "cheerleading" for globalization and free trade, the interconnectedness of the media system with the economic system all but eliminates the potential for substantive critique or oversight of corporate behavior. According to McChesney, "The largest media firms are members in good standing in the corporate community and closely linked through business relations, shared investors, interlocking directors, and shared political values with each other."[32] Such back-scratching was evidenced in media coverage of corporate scandals (e.g. Enron, WorldCom) from 2001–2003; while these scandals implicated system-wide corruption and malfeasance at the highest levels of business and government, the narrative of misbehaving individual CEOs (e.g. Ken Lay of Enron) dominated political and media discourse. Not only does such commercial bias provide the public with partial accounts of contemporary issues, but also contributes to the domination of economic rationality within the public sphere and the displacement of other forms of rationality (e.g. deliberation).[33]

Similar to this problem of commercial bias and exclusion, the intensity of competition for economic capital within the media field may create problems related to information quality. According to McChesney and Nichols, the prioritization of cost reduction (and subsequent maximization of profit) within commercial media has led to an increased reliance on press releases from "official sources" as raw material for news stories. This method of obtaining primary information causes the "range of legitimate debate" to be overly structured by the public relations capacities of existing power holders. Smaller media outlets (with less access to elite sources) adopt a similar strategy of reliance on wire services in lieu of actual journalists for basic reporting. In most instances, this lack of autonomous reporting manifests as a lack of independence between the media system and the political and economic systems; at its worst, however, such lack of independence borders on propaganda.[34]

The build-up to the 2003 invasion of Iraq by U.S.-led coalition forces is an example of such lack of media independence frequently cited by the authors.

In the relative absence of anti-invasion discourse among political elites, media coverage of the build-up lacked true viewpoint diversity; this is evidenced in part by a lack of scrutiny towards the various justifications for invasion, such as Colin Powell's testimony before the United Nations regarding weapons of mass destruction in Iraq.[35] Such lack of independence and skepticism was later addressed by a temporarily self-reflective media; a *New York Times* editorial published in 2004 specifically addressed a number of flaws in the paper's investigatory process. According to the *Times*,

> The problematic articles varied in authorship and subject matter, but many shared a common feature. They depended at least in part on information from a circle of Iraqi informants, defectors and exiles bent on "regime change" in Iraq, people whose credibility has come under increasing public debate in recent weeks... Complicating matters for journalists, the accounts of these exiles were often eagerly confirmed by United States officials convinced of the need to intervene in Iraq. Administration officials now acknowledge that they sometimes fell for misinformation from these exile sources...[36]

In addition to the reliance on non-credible experts, the *Times* editorial also identified a priority of speed over accuracy for the paper's competitiveness by being more interested in "rushing scoops into the paper" than "challenging reporters and pressing for more skepticism." As this example suggests, the desire to be more competitive *within* the field of commercial media may prompt elite media firms to adopt strategies which maximize revenues and other measures of market performance (e.g. circulation, ratings). However, such strategies also bring about a decline in the symbolic capital of media firms, primarily in the form of credibility, as the media cease to act as an engine for independent scrutiny of government actions (i.e. the fourth estate). Understood as such, competition between elite media firms and actors within the public sphere appears as an internally dynamic multipolar process, wherein the acquisition of symbolic capital through rationality and "excellence" exists alongside the competitive drive compelled by economic capital.[37] Such struggles for economic power (as viewership) and symbolic power (as influence) are not wholly internal to the elite realm, but rather necessarily involve interactions with other levels of the public sphere.

The Intermediate Public

In contrast to the highly competitive realm of the public elite, intermediate communicative activity is less likely to be competitive or guided by strategic concerns. While actors at the intermediate level may acquire a *moderate* quantity of visibility or authority in relation to segments or niches of the public, they are not necessarily in competition with elite level actors, as they are not sufficiently positioned to possess significant levels of public influence or to accrue any significant volume of capital. With this in mind, it becomes apparent that actors at the elite level and the intermediate level are effectively playing "different games"—that is to say, that they are involved in different processes with different goals. Communicative production emerging from the elite level contains the dual orientation of increasing or maintaining the symbolic capital stores of individual actors and reinforcing the larger social ordering on which elite differentiation is based. Actors at the intermediate level, however, engage in communicative production without such burdens.

The capacity of individuals outside of the elite realm to engage in communicative production with minimal perquisites or obligations is inextricably linked to the widespread usage of networked communications technologies; the virtual elimination of scarcity of information streams within the marketplace of networked communications as well as the ease of individual production and distribution of information streams facilitated by various online communications services and applications (e.g. blogs, YouTube, social media) have made a wide variety of non-elite forms of production and communication possible. The prevalence of such direct production and circulation underlies the common "new pamphleteer" analogy, which compares contemporary bloggers operating anonymously outside the institutional structures of professional media to 17th century pamphleteers, operating anonymously outside of regulatory governmental structures.[38]

Numerous varieties of text, audio, and video based applications are readily available for individuals with minimal skill to use for productive efforts, forming a kind of scaffolding upon which individual communicative production can be built. One of the more common formats for more structured, long-term communicative production is the blog. Given their multiplicity of variations as well as the constantly shifting nature of internet trends and practices, defining a blog is frequently considered a quixotic task. Google blog-publishing subsidiary Blogger.com defines a blog to new users as follows:

> Your blog is whatever you want it to be. There are millions of them, in all shapes and sizes, and there are no real rules. In simple terms, a blog is a web site, where you write stuff on an ongoing basis. New stuff shows up at the top, so your visitors can read what's new. Then they comment on it or link to it or email you. Or not.[39]

While the Blogger.com description lacks precision, it captures a number of the defining characteristics of blogs identified by journalist and new media entrepreneur Michael Conniff. According to Conniff, there are six characteristics of blogs which help differentiate them from static web-pages and conventional journalism pieces (e.g. columns, articles, etc.).

First, blogs organize entries in reverse chronological order (i.e. newest first); similarly, entries do not necessarily require a regular publishing schedule. Second, the content of blog entries is unfiltered; there are no intermediaries (e.g. editors) between the creator of the entry and the reader. Revising entries after publication is a common practice, but such changes are often made visible to the reader via strikethrough text. Third, blogs frequently contain comment fields or some other mechanism for interaction with both the creator of the entry and other readers. The fourth and fifth characteristics are links to websites, news articles, entries on other blogs, and common usage of block quoted text copied from these external sites. Finally, blog entries are frequently written with an irreverent, informal, or personal tone, in contrast with the objective and depersonalized tone of conventional journalism.[40] It is important to note that none of these characteristics are *sine qua non* for being considered a blog or for being comparatively successful; any combination of a few of these characteristics is often sufficient to be considered a blog and thus, something other than conventional journalism.

In and of itself, the existence of blogs as a mechanism for individual communication and expression outside of the structures of commercial mass media is significant; of even greater significance, however, is the potential for blogs to contribute to (political) discourse in the public sphere. Such potential for blog contributions usually occurs in two related, but conceptually distinct, patterns.

First, as personalized accounts of current events, blogs can provide alternative viewpoints and additional narrative content to media stories. While such personal journaling (i.e. "journal-blogs") risks veering towards narcissism and banality, under certain circumstances, personal journal-blogs can make unique and meaningful contributions to the public sphere.[41] One frequently discussed example of the unique contributions offered by blogs are the blogs of actively deployed military personnel, variously known as "soldier blogs," "warblogs," and/or "milblogs." Reaching their height of popularity (both in terms of authorship and readership) in 2004 and 2005, blogging offered deployed personnel a mechanism both for personal connectedness (i.e. communication with friends and loved ones via personal narratives) as well as to provide a raw, unfiltered perspective on on-the-ground conditions in Iraq and Afghanistan.[42]

In addition to giving citizens a better understanding of the daily life within a military engagement, milblogs also represented a mechanism for military personnel to offset biases or misrepresentations within mainstream media. In 2005, CNN executive Eason Jordan made public comments suggesting that journalists had been deliberately targeted by American forces in Iraq on various occasions. While these comments received little initial attention in national media, milbloggers heavily promoted criticism of Jordan's refusal to apologize for or clarify his statements and were able to provide eyewitness accounts demonstrating the inaccuracy of Jordan's accusations. Jordan resigned from CNN shortly after the controversy surrounding his remarks gained the attention of the mainstream media, citing a desire to prevent CNN's reputation from being "unfairly tarnished."[43]

In a second common pattern, blogs can act as a filtering mechanism, through which individuals (or editorial teams) intervene in the communications market—usually by targeting information streams from mainstream media grouped around specific topics (i.e. topic-oriented blogs). In addition to performing a filtering function, topic-oriented blogs can also serve a librarian function, where pieces and streams of information become organized, collated, and annotated to make individual information seeking more robust.[44] The range of such topic-oriented blogs obviously spans the range of collective interests; for some sense of perspective on the relative popularity of political blogs, of the 1.2 million blogs indexed by Technorati (an online blog searching and ranking service), "politics" is the fifth largest category of blogs, placing behind "living" (food, health, religion, etc.), "technology," "business," and "entertainment."[45]

Where the journal-style blog acts as a new form of journalistic expression, expanding the range of voices within the communications market, filter-style blogs serve as a mechanism for self-organization of the communications market. By aggregating content from mainstream media within a specific topic range, and drawing attention (and commentary) from the broader public, highly visible topic-oriented blogs serve as common focal points for communication and formation of communities of interest. According to Benkler,

> We observe the web developing an order—with high-visibility nodes, and clusters of thickly connected "regions" where groups of Web sites accredit each other by mutual referencing. The high-visibility Web sites provide points of condensation for informing individual choices, every bit as much as they form points of condensation for public discourse.[46]

As organization of information streams in the networked public thus emerges from individual activity on a voluntary and relatively ad hoc basis, rather than through any institutional, legal, or corporate structures, communicative power can be seen as being increasingly held by the public within the networked public sphere.[47]

Intermediate Production and the Media System

Such capacity for intermediate level production may additionally serve to improve individual agency within the political system by improving public discourse overall. As discussed previously, some of the most widely advanced arguments in favor of blogs and other new media applications relate to their capacity to disrupt the monopolization of information streams previously held—and to some degree, still held—by mainstream commercial media. Williams and Delli Carpini describe three effects of networked communications which disrupt the axis of control running between political elites and journalists:

First, the expansion of politically relevant media and the blurring of genres leads to a struggle within the media itself for the role of authoritative gatekeeper. Second, the expansion of media outlets, and the obliterating of the normal news cycle has created new opportunities for non-mainstream political actors to influence the setting and framing of the political agenda. And, third, this changed media environment has created new opportunities and pitfalls for the public to enter and interpret the political world.[48]

Two of these three effects—gatekeeping and agenda setting—merit more specific attention at this point.

One of the primary functions of journalists within the modern media system is to act as gatekeepers by selecting which news events and what information related to those events would be presented to the public. Under ideal circumstances, journalists' training and professional experience give them the capacity to make determinations regarding importance and public relevance.[49] However, within the contemporary media marketplace, competition between media firms and the imperative to remain profitable and advertiser-friendly place public interest decisions at risk of being secondary to economic decisions.[50] According to Strangelove, this creates an ironic situation in which the drive towards commercialization leads to a loss of audience: "Corporations create a demand for non-market sources of news when they pursue content and editorial standardizing strategies and erode journalistic autonomy in the name of cost cutting and vested interests."[51] This lack of perceived public interest, as well as a lack of transparency by journalists has contributed to a general public dissatisfaction with mainstream commercial media, and increasingly motivates individuals to seek political information from online sources.[52]

Enter political blogs. Political blog sites (e.g. Huffington Post, Politico, Red State) perform the conventional gatekeeping function of organizing and attributing some sense of relevance or importance to political information while simultaneously inviting more transparency and accountability via reader interaction. In addition, blogs may also (for better or worse) expand the range of "acceptable" topics for public presentation; as previously discussed, blogs frequently serve to draw attention to gossip and scandals that mainstream commercial media would not otherwise present for public consideration.[53]

Similar to gatekeeping, blogs frequently act as mechanisms for the hyper-scrutinization of both elected officials and media figures. Bolstered by high-profile scandals (e.g. Dan Rather's *memogate* scandal regarding the authenticity of President George W. Bush's service records, plagiarism by *New York Times* reporter Jayson Blair), as well as general dissatisfaction with mainstream media, the performance of surveillance on media figures is an increasingly common blog function.[54] Reynolds nicely summarizes this trend as follows:

Where before journalists and pundits could bloviate at leisure, offering illogical analysis or citing "facts" that were in fact false, now the Sunday morning op-eds have already been dissected on Saturday night, within hours of their appearing on newspapers' websites.[55]

Such scrutinization signals a breaking down of the monopolistic control over information held by major media firms, and more importantly, serves to draw into question both the mainstream media's ability to successfully make authoritative claims and to legitimately perform gatekeeping functions.[56] Empirical studies on blog content suggest that this activity of scrutinizing the mainstream media is highly popular, more so than actual independent journalism or firsthand reporting.[57]

The significance of the gatekeeping and watchdog functions performed by blogs is fairly straightforward: to the extent that the capacity to determine which information streams are given a prominent presentation before the public and which are given little to no presentation constitutes a form of power (i.e. media power[58]), any gains of such power by blogs represent a weakening of such power in commercial media. However, blogs and mainstream media do not exist in a completely antagonistic relationship. Bloggers (and the general public) need journalists and media institutions for reliable reporting, despite no longer wanting or needing commercial media to perform gatekeeping functions. This is not to say that journalists must merely chronicle events; rather, through new practices of transparency and interaction with readers, journalists can play an important role in helping readers navigate the complexities of ongoing public issues.[59]

Such interactions and contestations between mainstream commercial media and new media can be seen in the contemporary example of the vaccine-autism controversy. In 1998, a group of thirteen researchers led by Andrew Wakefield published a paper in British medical journal *The Lancet* which posited a relationship between MMR vaccination, gastrointestinal dysfunction, and autistic developmental disorders.[60] This paper, known colloquially as the "Wakefield report" caught the attention of mainstream media in Britain and the United States, prompting a public scare over safety of routine vaccinations.

After aggressive efforts by the medical community to calm the public, the debate over vaccine safety seemed to have gone dormant.[61] The controversy, however, was renewed in 2007 with the publication of comedienne and former model Jenny McCarthy's memoir, *Louder than Words: A Mother's Journey in Healing Autism*. McCarthy's controversial views on autism—that the development of autistic disorders is linked to ingredients in vaccines, and that special therapies and diets can help children "recover from" autistic disorders[62]—were promoted and reproduced with little or no contextualization vis-à-vis the dominant views of scientific and medical communities on a number of major media venues (e.g. *Oprah, Larry King Live, ABC News*). In one frequently cited example, ABC News ran a brief description of a study published in the journal *Pediatrics* which concluded that special diets had no efficacy in reducing or altering autistic behaviors. Within the one-minute clip, the summary of the *Pediatrics* article lasted eleven seconds, followed by thirty-two seconds of McCarthy's rebuttal and promotion of diet-based remedies for autism.[63]

This perceived unwillingness of mainstream media to adequately represent challenges to McCarthy, as well as the larger anti-vaccination movement, has prompted a groundswell of coverage within blogs (Discover Magazine's *Bad Astronomy* blog) and podcasts (*The Skeptics' Guide to the Universe*). Among such alternative forms of media and communication, a popular rejoinder to anti-vaccination arguments is the documentation of upswings in preventable diseases coinciding with the anti-vaccination movement.[64] One such website—jennymccarthybodycount.com—displays running counters of vaccine preventable illnesses and deaths since McCarthy's first public statements regarding vaccines. Through such media outlets, scientists, doctors, and interested members of the general public monitor the anti-vaccination movement in the realm of health care policy and the representation of anti-vaccination claims within media. In doing so, such communicative activities expand the available public dialogue regarding vaccinations, adding critical and expert voices that have previously been marginalized by mainstream media outlets.

Despite such examples of intermediate production serving as an external check against the outputs of elite level media firms, the overall reliance of new media on the output from mainstream media sources makes blogs often resemble *supplements to*—rather than *replacements for*—commercial media. Perhaps more disconcerting, such reliance may also paradoxically strengthen the position and authority of existing media firms. Based on a quantitative study of posts from leading political blogs, Reese et al. conclude that:

> [B]loggers, for the most part, simply engage the facts and information carried in news accounts, accepting them at face value and using them to form their own arguments, reinforce views, and challenge opponents. They rarely challenge specific reportorial techniques and larger media structures. We may thus regard them ironically as in some ways preserving and reinforcing professional norms of journalism as they disseminate content generated by traditional reporting practices.[65]

This tendency to reproduce the outputs of elite media firms—albeit in modified or commented form—suggests a relationship that is complex and interdependent, rather than simply antagonistic; various patterns of interaction between the elite and intermediate layers will be explored in more depth in Chapter 4.

The General Public

The diffusion of networked communication technologies and practices has not negated the existence of massified audiences; the passive reception of information streams produced by others is, and likely will continue to be, the primary activity for significant portions of any communications environment. Networked communications, however, have altered the general public's capacity for communicative activity, as well as the matrix of relationships and processes in which the general public exists.

As identified in Figure 3.1, the general public receives information from both intermediate and elite level sources in a wide variety of media formats. The presence of the intermediate public is highly significant for the general public, as such intermediate level production not only increases the number of information streams that the general public is exposed to, but also offers an alternative to elite level media firms. Through this relationship with the general public, the intermediate public may enhance processes of opinion-formation. Intermediate production may also, in concert with active consumption, produce new mechanisms for the public to articulate its preferences (see Figure 3.2). Such interactions between elite, intermediate, and general

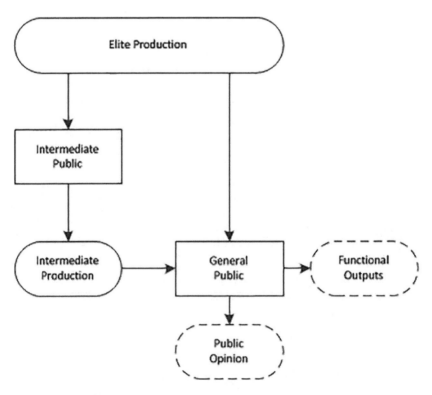

Figure 3.2 Conventional Public Output Processes

levels will be examined separately, through the lenses of "conventional" and "networked" output processes.

The processes of "conventional" public output are those traditionally associated with public opinion (broadly understood), as well as a variety of more specialized functional outputs. As one type of output, the public produces "public opinion" which, specific to the political public sphere, commonly occurs via opinion polling or similar mechanisms. Public opinion polls serve a broad function within the larger public sphere, in that they may represent inputs into a variety of other processes; they also possess a variety of limitations, however, not the least of which is that the terms of the opinion poll (i.e. the questions being asked) are *dictated to* the public, rather than being *determined by* the public. The public also produces "functional outputs," which link to specific processes within other areas. Relevant to the political public sphere, the most common functional output is voting; such voting may occur in the official electoral processes of the state or the internal processes of political parties or civic organizations. These outputs are "conventional" in the sense that the emergence of the intermediate public has little impact on the nature of the outputs themselves; voting and opinion polls played a significant role in the public sphere long before the development of networked communication.

In regard to conventional output processes, one of the most obvious effects of intermediate level production is a substantially increased amount of information available to individuals. Such increases in information streams, coupled with a weakened capacity for the media system to perform gatekeeping functions, produce a potential obstacle to opinion-formation processes through the risk of "information overload"; due to the massive amounts of information presented before the public (within both the networked communications environment and the media environment of the 24-hour news cycle) the resource cost for staying informed increases, as the responsibility for evaluating the relative value of any given information stream has been passed on to the information seeker. Contemporary research, however, suggests that information overload is not problematic, due to conventionally understood processes of opinion leadership.

Systematically developed by Katz and Lazarsfeld in 1955, the opinion leader idea holds that the flows of communications are mediated by individuals. According to the authors, this mediation forms a two-step flow whereby "ideas, often, seem to flow *from* radio and print *to* opinion leaders and *from them* to the less active sections of the population."[66] In serving as a link between information streams from a variety of media sources and those members of the public who might otherwise have more limited media exposure, opinion leaders serve a *relay function*. Contemporary empirical research drawn from the field of marketing studies suggests that opinion leaders in online environments share many characteristics with opinion leaders in offline environments.[67] Lyons and Henderson suggest that opinion leaders tend to curiously explore media of all formats, while non-leaders use media in more limited and instrumental patterns.[68] Relay functions appear to be significant within social networking environments as well; marketing research on word-of-mouth transmissions of information suggests that personal recommendations of new services are more significant to individual decision making than direct (i.e. not mediated through opinion leaders) transmission of information within online environments.[69] The point of this discussion is to suggest that networked communications have had little effect on conventional output processes; through networked communications, information is relayed from more active members of the public to those who are less active in a similar manner as that of mediated communications.

The General Public in the Networked Public Sphere

Of potentially more significance are new output processes facilitated by networked communication. Specifically, through the mechanism of active consumption, the general public possesses a capacity to articulate its preferences on its own terms, rather than on those structured via mechanisms of public opinion research. Given the sheer volume of communicative production (occurring both as intermediate production and active consumption) distributed over innumerable sites, communication is necessarily analyzed at the aggregate level. Various mechanisms and measures exist for tracking the volume of specific activities within the networked public, such as inbound traffic to websites (Alexa), the frequency of specific search engine terms (Google Trends), or hashtag usage in Twitter posts. A useful general concept in relation to such aggregate trends is "buzz," which effectively signifies a convergence or sustenance of trends; whenever the attention of the (normally) dispersed and fragmented public appears to be focused on the same topic at the same time, buzz occurs. According to Cornfeld et al., buzz serves as an accelerated mechanism for indicating public preferences and affecting the course of currently unfolding events; buzz can:

> embolden or embarrass its subjects. It can affect sales, donations, and campaign coffers. It can move issues up, down, and across institutional agendas (across being issue re-conceptualization or re-framing). When these changes occur, buzz can shift the balance of forces arrayed in a political struggle, and so affect its outcome.[70]

Figure 3.3 suggests that buzz emerges from what is effectively a production-and-feedback cycle between the intermediate public and the general public. Within this cycle, there is no clearly privileged position for leading or initiating buzz—both the intermediate public and the general public can act in leading capacities: through filtering and promoting specific news items or information streams, sites of intermediate production (e.g. blogs, message boards) serve as an engine of generating buzz independently of the agendas promoted by commercial media outlets; through mechanisms of active

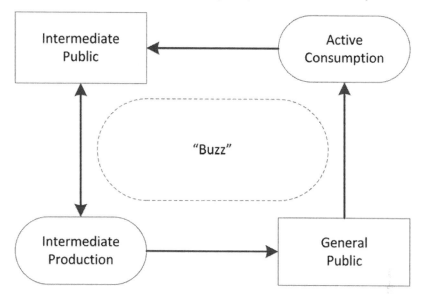

Figure 3.3 Networked Output Processes

consumption (especially social networking applications, such as Twitter), the general public independently signals its interests.

Thus, the potential benefit of such output is that it represents a bottom-up articulation of public interest or concern. Recall that in Habermas' revised model, the responsibility of detecting the "impulses" of the public falls on elite actors, with their ability to perform this function threatened by the economic imperatives of the media system.[71] By virtue of being articulated directly by the public itself, buzz can serve to transmit such impulses independently; any risk of potential intervention of the economic system is thus bypassed. While such "buzzmaking power" is not necessarily equivalent to the institutionally-grounded influence possessed by elite public actors, it nonetheless represents an independent mechanism for the public's self-articulation.

The Limitations of the General Public

This potential capacity for self-articulation, however, suffers from three serious limitations. First, the various mechanisms for measuring and detecting trends in the general public's communicative activity generally lack sufficient context to determine its larger significance. In other words, the relative frequency of what topics people are *discussing* does not necessarily signal *what positions* the public is taking on the topics they are discussing.

Second, and perhaps more importantly, the buzz-generating cycle represents a *compressed* form of opinion formation, which results from the accelerated nature of networked public communication. Acceleration in communication is not simply a function of the speed at which messages are transmitted and responded to, but is one iteration of broader social phenomena in which the longevity and stability of social practices and relationships are lessened by consistent and rapid change. According to Rosa and Scheuerman, under conditions of acceleration:

> [T]he lifeworld is constantly dismantled at an ever-faster velocity: fashions, lifestyles, product cycles, jobs, relations to spouses and sexual partners, political and religious beliefs, forms of practice and association, as well as particular orientations toward social action become increasingly contingent and unstable during the course of modernity.[72]

For the political system at large, the rapidity with which issues are formulated and articulated within public communication, constitutes, according to Bruce Bimber, a form of "accelerated pluralism," in which "issues develop and move more quickly because of the quicker cycle of mobilization and response, and in which government officials increasingly hear from and respond to new kinds of groups—those without large, stable memberships or affiliations with established institutions."[73] In one respect, a compressed opinion-formation cycle enables the public to "keep up" with the rapidity of issue development within the political system at large, thus maintaining the openness of public communication. However, within such a compressed cycle, reactive public opinions (i.e. knee-jerk reactions to issues) are privileged over more slowly developed opinions. Indeed, the very concept of buzz attaches significance to the communicative acts of the general public only at the moment they are initiated; any degree of reflexivity or consideration of issues over time on behalf of the public is simply unaccounted for.

A third, and perhaps more disturbing, limitation on the public's capacity for self-articulation is manipulation. Biases inherent in search engines represent a potential mechanism for manipulation of the information that individuals are exposed to, thus disrupting the production-feedback cycle shown in Figure 3.3 by privileging elite-level outputs over intermediate-level outputs. A more brazen form of manipulation exploits the anonymous and massified nature of networked communication for strategic intervention in opinion aggregation processes. Specifically, by creating fake online identities and mobilizing them within opinion aggregation processes, individuals can artificially "create the illusion of support for one's self, allies or company."[74] Termed "sock-puppeting," this phenomenon had, until recently, been evidenced primarily in relation to individual reputation management; in one prominent example, an editor at *The New Republic* was suspended for using a sock puppet on the magazine's website to harass readers who criticized his works.[75] However, contemporary controversies regarding "persona management" by both private corporations and various components of the

Department of Defense suggest that large-scale software automation of such usage of fake personas is on the rise.[76]

To the extent that the communicative actions of sophisticated computer-generated online personas cannot be distinguished from those of real users, the outputs of the general public risk becoming completely overrun by strategic interventions.[77] The potential for such manipulation, however, may be partially offset through various forms of government intervention. One such existing intervention is a Federal Trade Commission requirement that within online communications—blogs, in particular—endorsements of products must include disclosures of material interest; such regulation is intended to help consumers differentiate between potentially deceptive "word-of-mouth" marketing efforts and genuine individual reviews of products.[78] Another such initiative currently under development by the Obama administration is the National Strategy for Trusted Identities in Cyberspace; led by the U.S. Department of Commerce, this initiative is intended to create an identity credential system, applicable both to commercial and communicative environments.[79] To the extent that credentialed online identities are both utilized and recognized by the public, the usage of fake or managed online identities would substantially decrease.

Overall, while the cycle of communication between the intermediate public and the general public may be of mixed value for the self-articulation of the public, it seems highly compatible with Peters' conception of public culture. Specifically, the interactions between the intermediate public and the general public represent an open realm within which various aspects of public culture can be articulated and considered outside of the structures of the media system. Such open communication has frequently been observed in relation to popular culture (broadly understood). In relation to cultural works (e.g. music and films), production outside of the media system serves as a mechanism for individual creativity and experimentation. Perhaps more importantly, such culture production outside of the media system provides an opportunity for the public itself to determine the content of symbols in popular culture and to resist overt control of cultural meanings.[80]

Conclusion

Between these three layers of the networked public sphere, relationships of communication and communicative production are inherently complex, becoming even more so as struggles for influence and public attention transform into competition for recognition and symbolic power. What remains to be examined is the interrelation between the dynamics of communication and the dynamics of constraint—especially social constraint—within the networked public. The following chapter will attempt to illustrate such interrelations by looking at contemporary examples of constraint efforts.

Notes

1. Grossman, *The Electronic Republic: Reshaping Democracy in the Information Age*, 149.
2. Thompson refers to this as "mediated quasi-interaction." See Thompson, *The Media and Modernity: A Social Theory of the Media*, 81–3.
3. Benkler, *The Wealth of Networks: How Social Production Transforms Markets and Freedom*, 60.
4. Castells, *The Rise of the Network Society*, 71.
5. Poster, *Information Please: Culture and Politics in the Age of Digital Machines*, 195–6.
6. Jefferson, "Letter to the Marquis de La Fayette."
7. Jefferson, "Letter to Edward Carrington," 359.
8. Jefferson, "Second Inaugural Address."
9. Siebert, Peterson, and Schramm, *Four Theories of the Press*, 51.
10. Reynolds, *An Army of Davids: How Markets and Technology Empower Ordinary People to Beat Big Media, Big Government, and Other Goliaths*, 95–7.
11. See for example, Jenkins, *Convergence Culture: Where Old and New Media Collide*.
12. Benkler, *The Wealth of Networks: How Social Production Transforms Markets and Freedom*, 10–13.
13. Lessig, *Remix: Making Art and Commerce Thrive in the Hybrid Economy*, 28–9, 85.
14. Ibid., 59–60.
15. "The Web at 25."
16. Peters, "The Functional Capacity of Public Spheres," 125. Peters, "On Public Deliberation and Public Culture," 81–2. Peters, "The Meaning of the Public Sphere," 50–1.
17. The taxonomy of levels of communicative production presented in Table 3.1 is partially inspired by Gerhards and Schafer's discussion of different fora within the public sphere. The authors' presentation, however, suffers from a number of conceptual ambiguities, especially regarding their application of the concept of "organizational prerequisites" to new media, as well as their identification of search engines as communicative fora. Furthermore, as I have explained at various points in this chapter, the fusion of "old" and "new" media in the contemporary communications environment makes their combination necessary to some degree. Gerhards and Schäfer, "Is the Internet a Better Public Sphere? Comparing Old and New Media in the USA and Germany."
18. Such terminology, however, only signifies the format of communication, not its level of production; as communicative entities which take the format (and organizational structure) of blogs have over time gained levels of visibility and reach comparable to national media firms (e.g. the HuffingtonPost, DailyKos, RedState), the term no longer signifies a distinction from the media system. In other words, the important distinction lies in the level of production, not the mechanism or format of production. In terms of producing contributions to public discourse, it is the relative position of the producer which is ultimately significant. Benkler, *The Wealth of Networks: How Social Production Transforms Markets and Freedom*, Chapter 4.
19. Arthur, "What Is the 1% Rule?"
20. Indeed, according to Rodney Benson, one of the most significant aspects of the internet is its "reorganization" of competition within journalism and the media. Ubiquitous access to diverse forms of media via the internet effectively centralizes various media (e.g. newspapers, network newsrooms, blogs) into a single realm of competition. Benson, "News Media as a 'Journalistic Field': What Bourdieu Adds to New Institutionalism, and Vice Versa," 198.
21. Peters, "On Public Deliberation and Public Culture," 114–15.

22 Habermas, *Between Facts and Norms: Contributions to a Discourse Theory of Law and Democracy*, 375, 382.
23 Prestige, reputation, and public authority are alternative terms used by Peters to identify this component. His distinction between public authority and formal authority is functionally equivalent to the distinction between an-authority and in-authority discussed below. Peters, "On Public Deliberation and Public Culture," 100.
24 Peters uses the phrasing "institutional location and relevant social connections" to describe this factor. I have substituted the phrase "network positioning" for simplicity and better integration with other literatures. Peters, "On Public Deliberation and Public Culture," 100–1.
25 Peters, "The Meaning of the Public Sphere," 49.
26 Flathman, *The Practice of Political Authority: Authority and the Authoritative*, 16–18. See also Connolly, *The Terms of Political Discourse*, 112.
27 Friedman, "On the Concept of Authority in Political Philosophy," 91–2. In this essay, Friedman makes an interesting claim that, as superior knowledge of good and evil cannot be known, the application of an-authority to morality (e.g. the concept of moral authority) is vacuous.
28 Peters, "The Functional Capacity of Public Spheres," 131.
29 McChesney and Nichols, *The Death and Life of American Journalism: The Media Revolution That Will Begin the World Again*, 51.
30 Kellner, *Television and the Crisis of Democracy*, 9.
31 Herman, "The Media and Markets in the United States," 70–3.
32 McChesney, *The Political Economy of Media: Enduring Issues, Emerging Dilemmas*, 52. Edwin Baker argues that such conflicts of interest constitute a legal grounds for stricter FCC ownership regulations. See Baker, "Viewpoint Diversity and Media Ownership."
33 Dahlberg, "The Internet and Democratic Discourse: Exploring the Prospects of Online Deliberative Forums Extending the Public Sphere," 628.
34 McChesney and Nichols, *The Death and Life of American Journalism: The Media Revolution that Will Begin the World Again*, 44–6.
35 Ibid., 104–6. See also John Nichols and Robert Waterman McChesney, *Tragedy and Farce: How the American Media Sell Wars, Spin Elections, and Destroy Democracy* (New York: New Press, 2005).
36 "From the Editors: The Times and Iraq," *New York Times*, May 26, 2004.
37 Kaplan, *Politics and the American Press: The Rise of Objectivity, 1865–1920*, 6–7. Benson, "Shaping the Public Sphere: Habermas and Beyond," 178. Benson, "News Media as a 'Journalistic Field': What Bourdieu Adds to New Institutionalism, and Vice Versa," 189–90.
38 Kochan, "The Blogosphere and the New Pamphleteers." Moe, "Everyone a pamphleteer? Reconsidering comparisons of mediated public participation in the print age and the digital era."
39 "What's a Blog?"
40 Conniff, "Just What Is a Blog, Anyway?"
41 For example, a 2009 study by researchers at the Oxford University Press showed that gerund verbs (e.g. going, eating, watching, listening, reading, etc.) were among the most frequently used in messages on Twitter, suggesting that individuals most commonly use the service simply for documenting what they are doing at any given time. Purdy, "RT This: OUP Dictionary Team Monitors Twitterer's Tweets."
42 Memmott, "'Milbloggers' Are Typing Their Place in History." Hewitt, "Rise of the Milblogs."
43 Hockenberry, "The Blogs of War." Kurtz, "CNN's Jordan Resigns Over Iraq Remarks."

82   *The Contemporary Networked Public Sphere*

44 Perlmutter, *Blogwars*, 110–18.
45 "Technorati Blog Directory."
46 Benkler, *The Wealth of Networks: How Social Production Transforms Markets and Freedom*, 13, 172.
47 Grewal, *Network Power: The Social Dynamics of Globalization*.
48 Williams and Delli Carpini, "Unchained Reaction: The Collapse of Media Gatekeeping and the Clinton-Lewinski Scandal," 66.
49 Janowitz, "Professional Models in Journalism: The Gatekeeper and the Advocate," 618.
50 Brants and de Haan, "Taking the Public Seriously: Three Models of Responsiveness in Media and Journalism," 411.
51 Strangelove, *The Empire of Mind: Digital Piracy and the Anti-Capitalist Movement*, 176.
52 Tolbert and McNeal, "Unravelling the Effects of the Internet on Political Participation?" Gillmor, *We the Media: Grassroots Journalism by the People, for the People*, 6.
53 Hewitt, *Blog: Understanding the Information Reformation That's Changing Your World*, 6, 108.
54 Scott, "Pundits in Muckrakers' Clothing," 50.
55 Reynolds, *An Army of Davids: How Markets and Technology Empower Ordinary People to Beat Big Media, Big Government, and Other Goliaths*, 96.
56 Kahn and Kellner, "Technopolitics, Blogs, and Emergent Media Ecologies: A Critical/Reconstructive Approach," 29.
57 Kaye, "Blog Use Motivations: An Explanatory Study," 141.
58 This general definition corresponds to Habermas' conceptualization of media power in Habermas, "Political Communication in Media Society (2009)."
59 Gunter, *News and the Net*, 171–2. Gillmor, "Principles for a New Media Literacy."
60 Wakefield et al., "Retracted."
61 Fitzpatrick, *MMR and Autism: What Parents Need to Know*.
62 McCarthy and Carrey, "My Son's Recovery from Autism."
63 "Jenny McCarthy Dismisses Autism Study [VIDEO]."
64 For an example of a typical post, see Plait, "Measles Come Back, McCarthy's Revisionist History."
65 Stephen D. Reese et al., "Mapping the blogosphere: Professional and citizen-based media in the global news arena," *Journalism* 8, no. 3 (2007): 257.
66 Katz and Lazarsfeld, *Personal Influence: The Part Played by People in the Flow of Mass Communications*, 32.
67 See for example Dong and Zhang, "Ways of Identifying the Opinion Leaders in Virtual Communities." Zhou and Tsang, "Newsgroup Participants as Opinion Leaders and Seekers in Online and Offline Communications Environments."
68 Lyons and Henderson, "Opinion Leadership in a Computer-Mediated Environment."
69 Trusov, Bucklin, and Pauwels, "Effects of Word-of-Mouth Versus Traditional Marketing: Findings from an Internet Social Networking Site."
70 Cornfield et al., "Buzz, Blogs, and Beyond: The Internet and the National Discourse in the Fall of 2004."
71 Habermas, "Political Communication in Media Society (2009)," 77, 162.
72 Scheuerman and Rosa, "High Speed Society: Introduction," 5.
73 Bimber, "The Internet and Political Transformation: Populism, Community, and Accelerated Pluralism," 158.
74 Stone and Richtel, "The Hand That Controls the Sock Puppet Could Get Slapped."
75 Aspan, "New Republic Suspends an Editor for Attacks on Blog."

76 Monbiot, "The Need to Protect the Internet from 'Astroturfing' Grows Ever More Urgent." Storm, "Army of Fake Social Media Friends to Promote Propaganda." Hill, "Sarah Palin Should Have Hired HBGary to Create Her Virtual Army." Fielding and Cobain, "Revealed."
77 Thus, automated persona management represents a highly sophisticated form of "astroturfing"—artificially creating the appearance of citizen-based grassroots support for political issues.
78 "FTC Publishes Final Guides Governing Endorsements, Testimonials."
79 McCullagh, "Obama to Hand Commerce Dept. Authority over Cybersecurity ID." See also "National Strategy for Trusted Identities in Cyberspace."
80 Strangelove, *The Empire of Mind: Digital Piracy and the Anti-Capitalist Movement*, 132–3.

Bibliography

Arendt, Hannah. "What Is Authority?" In *Between Past and Future*. New York: Penguin Books, 1968.

Arthur, Charles. "What Is the 1% Rule?" *The Guardian*. July 20, 2006. www.guardian.co.uk/technology/2006/jul/20/guardianweeklytechnologysection2.

Aspan, Maria. "New Republic Suspends an Editor for Attacks on Blog." *The New York Times*. September 4, 2006. www.nytimes.com/2006/09/04/technology/04republic.html.

Baker, C. Edwin. "Viewpoint Diversity and Media Ownership." *Federal Communications Law Journal* 61, no. 3 (2009): 651–672.

Benkler, Yochai. *The Wealth of Networks: How Social Production Transforms Markets and Freedom*. New Haven, CT: Yale University Press, 2006.

Benson, Rodney. "Shaping the Public Sphere: Habermas and Beyond." *The American Sociologist* 40, no. 3 (July 2009): 175–197. doi:10.1007/s12108–12009–9071–9074.

Benson, Rodney. "News Media as a 'Journalistic Field': What Bourdieu Adds to New Institutionalism, and Vice Versa." *Political Communication* 23, no. 2 (2006): 187–202.

Bimber, Bruce. "The Internet and Political Transformation: Populism, Community, and Accelerated Pluralism." *Polity* 31, no. 1 (1998): 133–160.

Brants, Kees, and Yael de Haan. "Taking the Public Seriously: Three Models of Responsiveness in Media and Journalism." *Media, Culture & Society* 32, no. 3 (2010): 411–428.

Castells, Manuel. *The Rise of the Network Society*. 2nd edn. *The Information Age: Economy, Society, and Culture* 1. Malden, MA: Blackwell Publishers, 2010.

Conniff, Michael. "Just What Is a Blog, Anyway?" *Online Journalism Review*, September 29, 2005. www.ojr.org/ojr/stories/050929/.

Connolly, William E. *The Terms of Political Discourse*. 3rd edn. Princeton, NJ: Princeton University Press, 1993.

Cornfield, Michael, Jonathan Carson, Alison Kalis, and Emily Simon. "Buzz, Blogs, and Beyond: The Internet and the National Discourse in the Fall of 2004." *Pew Internet and American Life Project*, 2004. http://www.pewtrusts.org/uploadedFiles/wwwpewtrustsorg/News/Press_Releases/Society_and_the_Internet/PIP_Blogs_051605.pdf.

Dahlberg, Lincoln. "The Internet and Democratic Discourse: Exploring the Prospects of Online Deliberative Forums Extending the Public Sphere." *Information, Communication & Society* 4, no. 4 (2001): 615–633.

Dong, Dahai, and Xiaofei Zhang. "Ways of Identifying the Opinion Leaders in Virtual Communities." *International Journal of Business and Management* 3, no. 7 (2009): 21–27.

Fielding, Nick, and Ian Cobain. "Revealed: US Spy Operation That Manipulates Social Media." *The Guardian*, March 17, 2011, sec. Technology. www.theguardian.com/technology/2011/mar/17/us-spy-operation-social-networks.

Fitzpatrick, Michael. *MMR and Autism: What Parents Need to Know*. London: Routledge, 2004.

Flathman, Richard E. *The Practice of Political Authority: Authority and the Authoritative*. Chicago, IL: University of Chicago Press, 1980.

Friedman, Richard. "On the Concept of Authority in Political Philosophy." In *Authority*, edited by Joseph Raz, 56–91. New York: New York University Press, 1990.

"From the Editors: The Times and Iraq," *New York Times*, May 26, 2004.

"FTC Publishes Final Guides Governing Endorsements, Testimonials." Federal Trade Commission, 2009. http://ftc.gov/opa/2009/10/endortest.shtm.

Gerhards, Jürgen, and Mike S. Schäfer. "Is the Internet a Better Public Sphere? Comparing Old and New Media in the USA and Germany." *New Media Society* 12, no. 1 (2010): 143–160.

Gillmor, Dan. "Principles for a New Media Literacy." *Media Re:Public*, 2008. http://cyber.law.harvard.edu/sites/cyber.law.harvard.edu/files/Principles%20for%20a%20New%20Media%20Literacy_MR.pdf.

Gillmor, Dan. *We the Media: Grassroots Journalism by the People, for the People*. 1st edn. Sebastopol, CA: O'Reilly, 2004. www.oreilly.com/catalog/wemedia/book/.

Grewal, David Singh. *Network Power: The Social Dynamics of Globalization*. New Haven, CT: Yale University Press, 2008.

Grossman, Lawrence K. *The Electronic Republic: Reshaping Democracy in the Information Age*. New York: Viking, 1995.

Gunter, Barrie. *News and the Net*. Mahwah, NJ: L. Erlbaum, 2003.

Habermas, Jürgen. "Political Communication in Media Society: Does Democracy Still Have an Epistemic Dimension?" In *Europe, the Faltering Project*, 138–183. Malden, MA: Polity Press, 2009

Habermas, Jürgen. *Between Facts and Norms: Contributions to a Discourse Theory of Law and Democracy*. Cambridge, MA: MIT Press, 1996.

Herman, Edward. "The Media and Markets in the United States." In *The Right to Tell: The Role of Mass Media in Economic Development*, edited by Roumeen Islam. Washington, DC: The World Bank, 2002.

Hewitt, Hugh. *Blog: Understanding the Information Revolution That's Changing Your World*. Nashville, TN: T. Nelson Publishers, 2005.

Hewitt, Hugh. "Rise of the Milblogs," March 12, 2004. www.weeklystandard.com/Content/Public/Articles/000/000/003/840fvgmo.asp.

Hill, Kashmir. "Sarah Palin Should Have Hired HBGary to Create Her Virtual Army," February 23, 2011. http://blogs.forbes.com/kashmirhill/2011/02/23/sarah-palin-should-have-hired-hb-gary-to-create-her-virtual-army/.

Hockenberry, John. "The Blogs of War." *Wired*, August 2005. www.wired.com/wired/archive/13.08/milblogs_pr.html.

Janowitz, Morris. "Professional Models in Journalism: The Gatekeeper and the Advocate." *Journalism Quarterly* 52, no. 4 (1975): 618–662.

Jefferson, Thomas. "Letter to the Marquis de La Fayette." In *The Writings of Thomas Jefferson (Volume 15)*, 490–494. Washington, DC: Thomas Jefferson Memorial Association, 1823.

Jefferson, Thomas. "Second Inaugural Address." In *The Writings of Thomas Jefferson (Volume 3)*, 375–383. Washington, DC: Thomas Jefferson Memorial Association, 1805.

Jefferson, Thomas. "Letter to Edward Carrington." In *The Writings of Thomas Jefferson (Volume 4)*, 357–361. Washington, DC: Thomas Jefferson Memorial Association, 1787.

Jenkins, Henry. *Convergence Culture: Where Old and New Media Collide*. New York: New York University Press, 2006. www.loc.gov/catdir/toc/ecip069/2006007358.htm lhttp://www.loc.gov/catdir/enhancements/fy0730/2006007358-d.htmlhttp://www.loc.gov/catdir/enhancements/fy0733/2006007358-b.html.

"Jenny McCarthy Dismisses Autism Study [VIDEO]," January 2010. http://abcnews.go.com/video/playerIndex?id=9477472.

Kahn, Richard, and Douglas Kellner. "Technopolitics, Blogs, and Emergent Media Ecologies: A Critical/Reconstructive Approach." In *Small Tech: The Culture of Digital Tools*, 22–37. Minneapolis, MN: University of Minnesota Press, 2008.

Kaplan, Richard L. *Politics and the American Press: The Rise of Objectivity, 1865–1920*. Cambridge: Cambridge University Press, 2002.

Katz, Elihu, and Paul Felix Lazarsfeld. *Personal Influence: The Part Played by People in the Flow of Mass Communications*. Foundations of Communications Research. Glencoe, Ill: Free Press, 1955.

Kaye, Barbara. "Blog Use Motivations: An Explanatory Study." In *Blogging, Citizenship, and the Future of Media*, edited by Mark Tremayne, 127–148. London: Routledge, 2007.

Kellner, Douglas. *Television and the Crisis of Democracy. Interventions–Theory and Contemporary Politics*. Boulder, CO: Westview Press, 1990.

Kochan, Donald J. "The Blogosphere and the New Pamphleteers." *Nexus Law Journal* 11 (2006): 99–109.

Kurtz, Howard. "CNN's Jordan Resigns Over Iraq Remarks," February 12, 2005. www.washingtonpost.com/wp-dyn/articles/A17462-2005Feb11.html.

Lessig, Lawrence. *Remix: Making Art and Commerce Thrive in the Hybrid Economy*. New York: Penguin Press, 2008.

Lyons, Barbara, and Kenneth Henderson. "Opinion Leadership in a Computer-Mediated Environment." *Journal of Consumer Behaviour* 4, no. 5 (2005): 319–329.

McCarthy, Jenny, and Jim Carrey. "My Son's Recovery from Autism." *Turner Broadcasting System*, April 2008. http://articles.cnn.com/2008-04-02/us/mccarthy.autsimtreatment_1_autism-evan-hannah-poling?_s=PM:US.

McChesney, Robert Waterman. *The Political Economy of Media: Enduring Issues, Emerging Dilemmas*. New York: Monthly Review Press, 2008. www.loc.gov/catdir/toc/ecip0822/2008027102.html.

McChesney, Robert Waterman, and John Nichols. *The Death and Life of American Journalism: The Media Revolution That Will Begin the World Again*. Philadelphia, PA: Nation Books, 2010.

McCullagh, Declan. "Obama to Hand Commerce Dept. Authority over Cybersecurity ID," January 7, 2011. http://news.cnet.com/8301-31921_3-20027800-281.html?tag=contentMain;contentBody.

Memmott, Mark. "'Milbloggers' Are Typing Their Place in History." *USA Today*, May 11, 2005. www.usatoday.com/news/world/iraq/2005-05-11-milblogs-main_x.htm.

Moe, H. "Everyone a pamphleteer? Reconsidering comparisons of mediated public participation in the print age and the digital era." *Media, Culture & Society* 32, no. 4 (July 2010): 692–700. doi:10.1177/0163443710367715.

Monbiot, George. "The Need to Protect the Internet from 'Astroturfing' Grows Ever More Urgent," February 23, 2011. www.guardian.co.uk/environment/georgemonbiot/2011/feb/23/need-to-protect-internet-from-astroturfing.

"National Strategy for Trusted Identities in Cyberspace." Washington, DC: The White House, 2011. www.whitehouse.gov/sites/default/files/rss_viewer/NSTICstrategy_041511.pdf.

Nichols, John and Robert Waterman McChesney, *Tragedy and Farce: How the American Media Sell Wars, Spin Elections, and Destroy Democracy*. New York: New Press, 2005.

Perlmutter, David D. *Blogwars*. Oxford; New York: Oxford University Press, 2008.

Peters, Bernhard. "The Functional Capacity of Public Spheres." In *Public Deliberation and Public Culture*, edited by Hartmut Wessler, 121–133. New York: Palgrave Macmillan, 2002.

Peters, Bernhard. "On Public Deliberation and Public Culture." In *Public Deliberation and Public Culture*, 68–118. New York: Palgrave Macmillan, 1997.

Peters, Bernhard. "The Meaning of the Public Sphere." In *Public Deliberation and Public Culture*, 33–67. New York: Palgrave Macmillan, 1994.

Plait, Phil. "Measles Come Back, McCarthy's Revisionist History." *Bad Astronomy*, 2010. http://blogs.discovermagazine.com/badastronomy/2010/05/26/measles-comes-back-mccarthys-revisionist-history/.

Poster, Mark. *Information Please: Culture and Politics in the Age of Digital Machines*. Durham, NC: Duke University Press, 2006.

Purdy, Christian. "RT This: OUP Dictionary Team Monitors Twitterer's Tweets," June 4, 2009. http://blog.oup.com/2009/06/oxford-twitter/.

Reese, Stephen, L. Rutigliano, K. Hyun, and J. Jeong. "Mapping the blogosphere: Professional and citizen-based media in the global news arena," *Journalism* 8, no. 3 (2007): 35–61.

Reynolds, Glenn H. *An Army of Davids: How Markets and Technology Empower Ordinary People to Beat Big Media, Big Government, and Other Goliaths*. Nashville, TN: Nelson Current, 2006. www.loc.gov/catdir/toc/ecip065/2005036710.htm lhttp://www.loc.gov/catdir/enhancements/fy0623/2005036710-d.html.

Scheuerman, William E., and Hartmut Rosa. "High Speed Society: Introduction." In *High Speed Society*, edited by William E. Scheuerman and Hartmut Rosa, 1–32. University Park, PA: Pennsylvania State University, 2009.

Scott, D. Travers. "Pundits in Muckrakers' Clothing." In *Blogging, Citizenship, and the Future of Media*, edited by Mark Tremayne, 39–57. London: Routledge, 2007.

Siebert, Fred S., Theodore Peterson, and Wilbur Schramm. *Four Theories of the Press*. Freeport, NY: Books for Libraries Press, 1973.

Stone, Brad, and Matt Richtel. "The Hand That Controls the Sock Puppet Could Get Slapped." *New York Times*. July 16, 2007.

Storm, Darlene. "Army of Fake Social Media Friends to Promote Propaganda," February 23, 2011. www.pcworld.com/article/220495/army_of_fake_social_media_friends_to_promote_propaganda.html.

Strangelove, Michael. *The Empire of Mind: Digital Piracy and the Anti-Capitalist Movement*. Toronto: University of Toronto Press, 2005.
"Technorati Blog Directory," n.d. http://technorati.com/blogs/directory/.
"The Web at 25." *Pew Research Center*, February 2014. www.pewinternet.org/files/2014/02/PIP_25th-anniversary-of-the-Web_0227141.pdf.
Thompson, John B. *The Media and Modernity: A Social Theory of the Media*. Stanford, CA: Stanford University Press, 1995.
Tolbert, Caroline J., and Ramona S. McNeal. "Unravelling the Effects of the Internet on Political Participation?" *Political Research Quarterly* 56, no. 2 (2003): 175–185.
Trusov, Michael, Randolph E. Bucklin, and Koen Pauwels. "Effects of Word-of-Mouth Versus Traditional Marketing: Findings from an Internet Social Networking Site." *Journal of Marketing* 73 (2009): 90–102.
Wakefield, A. J., A. Anthony, J. Linnell, D. M. Casson, M. Malik, M. Berelowitz, A. P. Dhillon, M. A. Thomson, P. Harvey, and others. "Ileal-lymphoid-nodual hyperplasia, non-specific colitis, and pervasive developmental disorder in children." *The Lancet* 351, no. 9103 (1998): 637–641.
"What's a Blog?," n.d. www.blogger.com/tour_start.g.
Williams, Bruce A., and Michael X. Delli Carpini. "Unchained Reaction: The Collapse of Media Gatekeeping and the Clinton-Lewinski Scandal." *Journalism* 1, no. 1 (2000): 61–85.
Zhou, Nan, and Alex Tsang. "Newsgroup Participants as Opinion Leaders and Seekers in Online and Offline Communications Environments." *Journal of Business Research* 58, no. 9 (2005): 1186–1193.

4 Constraint in the Networked Public

Introduction

The elite stratum, from all perspectives examined in this project, operates on a self-regulating basis. Exclusivity and stratification structure a competitive environment in which violations of acceptability will be brought before the public eye. Such self-regulation, however, is neither imperfect nor wholly disinterested. As such, the public's ire represents a second line of defense against unacceptable elite actions, most commonly as a prompt for the mobilization of competing elites. Based on the concepts developed in the preceding chapters, a third line of defense exists in the form of elite constraint, wherein the public itself not only identifies and reacts to unacceptable elite actions, but utilizes mechanisms of constraint on a punitive basis.

The distinction between competitive elitism and constrained elitism is worth briefly rearticulating. Through the first process, the grievances of the public become part of the theatricality of "normal" political competition; the various segments of the public form a grand reserve army, whose sentiments acquire significance only when considered strategically useful to one side or the other in symbolic conflict. Processes of constraint, however, represent efforts for the public to act on its own behalf, intervening in and disrupting normal patterns of elite competition. Thus, in considering the role of networked communications within contemporary elite/non-elite interactions, care must be taken to observe that the increased capacity for communicative production available within intermediate public spaces does not necessarily entail constraint efforts; rather, it is equally plausible that reactive communicative actions emerging organically from intermediate public spaces become integrated into pre-existing lines of elite competition (i.e. normalized). Whether negative public sentiments become normalized or crystallize into a constraint attempt is primarily dependent upon the nature and context of the public's response, rather than the communicative means through which these demands are articulated. The following section introduces a general model of such responses.

A General Model of Public Reaction

Most instances of political decision making and public administration fail to capture the attention of the general public, owing to both political apathy and the inherent banality of the rational-bureaucratic state. This tendency coincides with the public's inherently reactive nature. While the public may have difficulty articulating its concerns on its own terms, it is highly capable of expressing a negative reaction under certain circumstances; the remainder of this section identifies the conditions under which the public becomes reactive, as well as the possibility of constraint efforts emerging.

Catalyzing the Public

Within the cacophony of the contemporary media system, some events seem to gain the public's attention more than others: the inherently dramatic nature of natural disasters (and their subsequent rescue efforts) tends to capture the public's interest, while other events, such as random acts of public violence, may prompt a strong emotional interest based on sympathy or fear. Regardless of the reason, some events serve to create a public focus by displacing other potential issues from the public's agenda.

Apart from being interesting or tragic, such events often serve to reveal an underlying problem or illustrate a deficiency within the status quo in regard to an issue that had previously been ignored, unseen, or portrayed as resolved. Such events (i.e. triggering events) serve to both focus the attention of segments of the public and prompt a demand for some kind of corrective action that will prevent or minimize the possibility of similar events in the future.

The reactive nature of the public may also become activated by actions or decisions made by elite actors, usually as a response to some policy change or statement regarding a public issue. Public reactions to elite actions are fairly straightforward. If segments of the public agree with or are impartial to changes initiated by elites, they will remain passive; if segments disagree with changes initiated by elites, they will demand some kind of corrective or reversal. On the whole, public reactivity to elite actions will occur more commonly than to triggering events; this is partially explained by the internal diversity of the public, as any elite action is likely to be rejected by some groups or segments. Furthermore, the multipolar nature of the elite realm makes nearly all aspects of the lifeworld subject to change through elite actions; the public is thus given more numerous opportunities for negative reactivity through elite actions than through triggering events.

Public Demands

Once a situation emerges in which segments of the public express a negative reaction, the existence and nature of the public's demands for correction or

90 Constraint in the Networked Public

redress must be considered. In instances of negative reactivity to elite actions, public demands will likely be narrowly tailored to the offending action in question: improper remarks can be corrected by apologies, disliked policy changes can be reversed, etc. In regard to triggering events, however, the range of potential public demands is much greater and significantly dependent upon the nature of the triggering event itself (see Figure 4.1).

Triggering events may possess similarities to previously considered political issues. In such instances, individuals within the public are likely to have already formed opinions on these topics, and elites are highly likely to have staked out positions on these issues (especially through party platforms) and (when applicable), settled into "issue camps." When such similarities exist, elite political actors have an interest in casting the event in terms of existing public issue camps, as a means of mobilizing previously acquired symbolic capital. This is especially important for the institutionalized components of political issue camps (e.g. political parties, interest groups), as the maintenance of their symbolic power depends in no small part on continuously reminding the public of the importance of their existence. While these types of events are likely to increase the visibility and perceived importance of a particular issue, they are unlikely to prompt the introduction of new corrective demands. Rather, public reactivity becomes a force of galvanization, wherein those members of the public who were previously unsure, undecided, or uninteresting in a particular issue are pressed to align themselves with an existing issue camp (i.e. to "choose a side"). Triggering events of

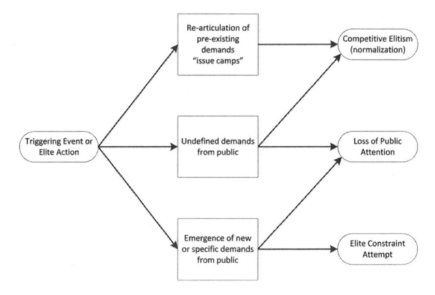

Figure 4.1 Modeling Public Demands

this type represent a nearly perfect form of "normalization," as the negative reactions of the public become channeled into existing competitive processes; when new policies eventually emerge, they do so as the result of internal forces *within* the elite realm, rather than constraint efforts.

Triggering events, however, may also introduce "new" or "novel" public issues; if the nature and circumstances of the event are sufficiently different from previous related or similar events, the re-articulation of existing issue positions becomes increasingly difficult, thus reducing the likelihood of normalization. Such instances of new issues may emerge from significant changes in various aspects of the lifeworld (e.g. the appearance of new diseases, development of new technologies, significant environmental changes), or may re-emerge as previously dormant issues (or issues of significantly limited applicability) become relevant to the larger public once again. To the extent that taking a firm stand on a new or uncertain issue represents a risk to their overall stores of symbolic capital, elite actors may adopt cautious strategies in their public statements on such issues, creating opportunities for the emergence of new demands from *outside* of the elite realm.

It is in such instances, where competing elite actors and institutions strategically ignore (or otherwise fail to normalize) a negative public reaction to triggering events, that the communicative-productive capacities within intermediate public spaces are most significant. In the face of a new public issue or problem, about which existing public actors and institutions have failed to sufficiently manage public sentiments, the outputs of the intermediate public will have a greater likelihood of impact in both the opinion-formation processes of the general public and the competitive processes of the elite realm.

The existence of a new or novel triggering event is not, in itself, enough to guarantee the emergence of a constraint effort. When triggering events activate new or dormant grievances, the public may be capable of expressing a negative reaction without necessarily articulating specific demands. Furthermore, the nature of the problem may be such that no specific demand or set of demands appears sufficient; overly complex issues may instead lead to the emergence of a multiplicity of concerns or demands. In such instances, where public dissatisfaction *does not* lead to the organic emergence of specific demands, public dissatisfaction is very likely to either be integrated into normal politics, or to simply dissipate as public attention shifts elsewhere.

Whether a triggering event prompts processes of normal elite competition or an attempt at elite constraint depends primarily on the nature of the event itself; if elite actors are unable to integrate public dissatisfaction into existing issue camps, or simply choose to downplay or ignore it, there is a possibility of such reactivity expanding into a constraint effort. The following sections address these two processes (integration and expansion) in greater detail, with a particular emphasis on the potential role of communicative production in the intermediate public.

Normalization and Integration

In their widely cited 2000 manuscript *Politics as Usual*, Michael Margolis and David Resnick provided a sober assessment of the transformative potential of networked communications; in contrast to much of the advocacy and speculative writing published in the late 1990s, Margolis and Resnick argued that the internet was no longer an experimental social frontier, but instead had become *normalized*. According to the authors,

> [T]hose who have been powerful in the past—the established organizations, the wealthy, and the privileged—are moving into cyberspace and taking their advantages with them. Whatever new exposure minor parties and movements have gotten by entering cyberspace has yet to be translated into real-world shifts of power and resources.[1]

This concept of normalization is highly relevant for understanding public reactivity in the context of networked communications. The widespread availability of networked communications and the communicative-productive tools which structure intermediate public spaces *should* create a significant potential for disruption of existing elite/non-elite relations. Certainly, this is true in limited circumstances, however, as the concept of normalization suggests, most of the communicative-productive capacity of networked communications is ultimately directed towards "ordinary politics and commercial activity."[2]

Normalization is thus the conventionally understood competitive process within a plural-elitist framework; while the intermediate public and general public play a role in such competition, their role ultimately facilitates elite processes, rather than disrupting them. Under normalization, the fundamental political status quo has not been altered. The basic lines of contestation between issue camps have not changed, the "excluded" voices remain in the dark, the individuals and groups who are relevant remain relevant. This is not to say, however, nothing changes; policy decisions and electoral outcomes change as part of the regular flow of competition. This is also not to say that the intermediate public is excluded, but rather that it becomes integrated into existing competitive processes.

As discussed in previous chapters, elite actors within the public realm must compete to gain the support of organized and unorganized groups and leverage such support towards specific political goals (e.g. defeating a particular piece of legislation); actors who successfully construct group interests and realize them through the various mechanisms of the state can gain significant quantities of symbolic capital.

Maintaining a competitive advantage in such a system depends primarily upon an elite actor's capacity to "sense" the waxing and waning of group constructions within the broader populace. Prior to the rise of the networked public, civil society organizations played a significant role in this competitive process. Consistent with de Tocqueville's maxim that "in democratic countries the science of association is the mother science," an organization's relative size of membership and store of resources exists as a proxy measure of the organization's overall importance within the public realm. Courting civil society organizations is an essential component of normal elite competition: candidates for office vie for group endorsements, public figures seek to book appearances at organization conventions, etc.

Civil society organizations, however, introduce a variety of problems related to the construction of group identities and interests. Once organized, group identities and interests begin to take on a fixed character; while such fixity may represent a secure source of support for elite actors, it also limits the net fluidity of group constructions available. The use of symbolic power within the public realm necessarily involves the continuous making and remaking of group identities; to the extent that they effectively freeze identities and interests, civil society organizations can only be temporarily or partially "useful" for competing elite agents. As Bourdieu writes, political organizations possess an inherent contradiction between the forces of "expression and representation" which give birth to groups, and the "mechanical logic of the apparatus" which groups must adopt as they become institutionalized.[3]

Because of such limitations, the emergence of groups within the intermediate public space represents a highly significant opportunity for elite actors to seek new constituencies. However, as groups within the intermediate public are generally self-constituting based on existing shared interests or normative commitments, elite actors seeking to establish their authenticity must do so on the group's own terms. This is inherently a risky strategy, as the support of the intermediate public cannot be "bought off" or otherwise granted through the kind of long-term institutional commitments more commonly made with actual organizations. Furthermore, as groups in the intermediate public lack any organizational resources, there are little to no guarantees of future forms of support.

The significance of the intermediate public for elite competition is greatest in instances of public dissatisfaction or reactivity where existing issue camps are not relevant and no new demands have materialized. In such instances, elite actors may attempt to identify and "integrate" pockets of dissatisfaction into the normal competitive process by modifying existing organizations or formulating new constituencies. Integration is not simply co-optation, however, as it is usually very beneficial to individuals in the intermediate public as well; through intermediate public structures, citizens can have greater non-massified interactions with elites and develop a heightened sense of political efficacy in relation to issues they are passionate about.

FiveThirtyEight—Integration in the Media System

The relationships between the intermediate and elite levels of the public sphere are often interdependent in nature; elite actors may look for strategic opportunities at the intermediate level, and intermediate level actors may seek to develop sufficient quantities of economic and symbolic capital (as influence) to move into the elite level. This mutually beneficial process of integration can be readily seen in the realm of publishing, following a fairly intuitive pattern. First, a blog or website (representing either an individual actor, or a collaborative effort) begins in relative obscurity, targeting a specialized or niche audience. Due to both the low economic cost of starting a blog and the closer proximity to the lifeworld of the general public, production at the intermediate level will reflect a wide variety of interests, grievances, and audiences that have otherwise been ignored or underrepresented by elite production. Having found such an audience, the website gains a following over time, eventually attracting the attention of actors at the elite level. Seeking to increase their own influence or audience, elite actors begin to associate with such "rising stars" within the intermediate level, culminating in various forms of institutional connection, such as contracts or other legal agreements.

One example of the integrative process can be seen through Nate Silver, and his blog FiveThirtyEight. A baseball statistician by trade, Silver began pseudonymously publishing mathematically-derived electoral analyses and predictions during the 2008 Democratic primary elections.[4] The accuracy of Silver's predictions drove substantial traffic to his blog, eventually leading to frequent "expert" appearances on national news media. The integration process reached its culmination in June 2010, with the announcement that Silver's blog would become a part of *The New York Times*' website.[5] In this instance, integration resulted through a combination of all three factors: authority via the accuracy of Silver's analysis, visibility through increased web traffic, and network position by gaining the attention of high-profile media outlets. While Silver's story represents an atypical case of integration—the overwhelming majority of such efforts will gain little to no visibility—it nonetheless demonstrates the process through which production in the intermediate public can rise to the elite level. Integrative action thus represents a path through which the deficiencies of the media system can be corrected, and the number of public actors who "emerge" from the public can be increased.

Perhaps ironically however, the impetus behind Silver's decision to start conducting political analyses was the perceived unsophistication of electoral analyses within the mainstream media.[6] Such a sentiment—that the media system gets stories wrong, excludes viewpoints, demonstrates biased gatekeeping, or otherwise fails to satisfy the public—represents a commonly and diffusely held negative reaction to the contemporary media system. By successfully integrating FiveThirtyEight on an institutional level, the *New York Times* validated and normalized this negative sentiment, creating a competitive advantage for itself in the process.

Constraint

In contrast to instances where a triggering event or elite action can be integrated into pre-existing issue camps or positions by elite actors, instances in which a new public issue, grievance, or demand emerges may develop into a constraint effort. As shown in Table 4.1, the defining characteristic of constraint efforts is that determination of whether or not an elite action is acceptable as well as the means of sanctioning (i.e. punishing) the offending elite is undertaken by the public itself; the public grievances and/or demands that emerge in the wake of a triggering event or elite action *do not* become part of regular elite competition. This lack of normalization may occur for a variety of reasons. The triggering event itself or the public demands for redress may be so far outside of the contemporary public agenda that existing issue positions are not applicable. Consistent with the concept of exclusion (as discussed in Chapter 3), a freshly articulated demand related to an existing issue may simply be ignored by elite actors for fear of re-kindling latent political grievances. Additionally, the public's demands following a triggering event may be insufficiently defined or simply too impractical for elite actors to integrate. Regardless of the reason behind the lack of normalization, its absence may allow a public grievance to develop into a constraint effort, or to simply fizzle out as the public's attention goes elsewhere. The following series of examples illustrate various scenarios in which public reactivity does or does not successfully lead to elite constraint.

Kony 2012—Ambiguous Demands and Public Reactivity

In March 2012, non-profit organization, Invisible Children, released a thirty minute short film (*Kony 2012*) describing the activities of African militia group the *Lord's Resistance Army* (LRA), emphasizing the use of child soldiers and the brainwashing tactics of the group's leader, Joseph Kony. Released on multiple video sharing and social networking sites, *Kony 2012* was viewed over 35 million times in less than one week; the video gained a massive amount of media attention within a relatively short time period, in part, by attracting the interest of a number of high profile celebrities.

Throughout the video, Invisible Children advocates for a more active role of the United States government in the arrest of Joseph Kony; according to

Table 4.1 Regulation of Elite Behaviors

Model	Unacceptable Action Determined by	Sanction Applied by
"Pure" Self-Regulation	Elite Norms	Competing Elites
Competitive Elitism (Normalization)	Public/Non-Elites	Competing Elites
Elite Constraint	Public/Non-Elites	Public/Non-Elites

the content of the video, if the U.S. would provide sufficient support personnel to the government of Uganda (the LRA's primary location) and apply greater political pressure, Kony would be arrested. Such an outcome has failed to be realized because not enough people in America know about Kony and the LRA. The video concludes with an exhortation for viewers to increase the visibility of Kony and the LRA, in order to prompt action by elected officials:

> He's not famous. He's invisible. Joseph Kony is invisible. Here is how we're going to make him visible. We are going to make Joseph Kony a household name—not to celebrate him but to bring his crimes to the light ... Our goal is to change the conversation of our culture and get people to ask, "Who is Joseph Kony?"[7]

Part of the effort to "Make Kony Famous" outlined in the video was a planned event in which supporters were encouraged to hang Kony-related signage within their communities on the night of April 19; anyone yet unaware of Kony/LRA, according to Invisible Children, would wake to find their familiar lived spaces disrupted by these messages, and would naturally seek out more information.

In terms of the rapid increase in visibility for this previously obscure issue, *Kony 2012* was a resounding success, passing over 100 million views in a record-setting six days.[8] Directly citing the popularity of the video and its impact among young people, Delaware Senator Chris Coons introduced a bipartisan resolution condemning Kony/LRA less than three weeks after the video's debut.[9] However, beyond this phenomenal speed of its viral spread, *Kony 2012* demonstrated a mixed legacy. Sen. Coons' resolution was unanimously passed in August 2012, signifying a continued recognition of the public's concerns; the resolution, however, was merely a restatement of existing U.S. policies.[10] As recently as 2009, Congress had authorized personnel and financial support to the Ugandan government for eliminating the LRA; as it did not contain any real policy change or actual legal authority, the 2012 resolution can ultimately be seen as an empty gesture. By the time of the planned "Cover the Night" event in April 2012, much of the buzz surrounding Kony/LRA appeared to have dissipated, with news sources from most major cities reporting little to no participation.[11] As of the time of this writing, Invisible Children has announced plans to dissolve its organization due to declines in funding.[12] The United States continues to provide assistance and support to the Ugandan government in fighting the LRA and stabilizing the region, but Joseph Kony himself has not been arrested.

The *Kony 2012* example provides rich material for analysis within a wide variety of academic subject areas (e.g. viral marketing, communication studies, etc.), but for the purposes of this book, it illustrates two significant aspects of constraint processes. The first is the significance of the public demand. As portrayed in the *Kony 2012* video, the unacceptable condition of the status quo is the continued free movement of Joseph Kony; the status quo can be made acceptable through Kony being arrested (i.e. brought to justice). This formulation, however, is fairly distant from any discrete actions that can be undertaken by or attributed to specific elite actors.

The second significant aspect of this example is the role of the intermediate public. The rapid spread of the *Kony 2012* video through the communicative structures of the intermediate public demonstrates the tremendous capacity of intermediate-level production (more specifically, active consumption) to increase the visibility of issues and issue positions. Through active consumption (in the spaces of the intermediate public), interested members of the public can perform a proto-activist function with virtually no resource costs or commitments. This aspect of the networked public is sometimes referred to pejoratively as "slacktivism." Individuals who are interested in a particular issue join message boards, use hashtags, or retweet interesting links; in doing so, they gain a sense of self-satisfaction for having "done something" about their issue. Such proto-activism, however, ultimately serves to weaken the capacity of civil society organizations or other forms of political organization, as the desire for people to "do something" has been displaced. Individuals do not feel compelled to become a dues-paying member of an organization, as talking about that organization on Facebook is good enough; never attending a party meeting or group rally is fine, so long as you help "get the word out" by retweeting the information about these events. Such proto-activism, however, may be beneficial by increasing the visibility and perception of relative importance of a particular issue. Creating sufficient buzz about an issue (or potential solution to an issue) may create sufficient opportunities for political entrepreneurship and/or strategic intervention by elite actors.

Such successful conversion from online buzz to actual opportunities for change, however, *requires* an achievable set of demands. Without the stipulation of a discrete action, which can be accomplished by and attributed to specific elite actors, there is no possibility of actual changes in elite actions or behaviors. The *Kony 2012* example nicely illustrates this requirement. No specific elite actor or institution could simply arrest Joseph Kony, nor was any specific actor or institution preventing his arrest or advocating his continued freedom; under these conditions, there were simply no actions available for elite actors to take, or unacceptable actions to constrain. The Kony example thus illustrates that in the absence of a clear formulation of how to re-establish an acceptable status quo, the public's reactivity is unsustainable; for a sustained constraint effort to emerge, the public must have an unambiguous understanding of what it is reacting against and what it expects to be done. The more distant or abstract the object of public reactivity, the more likely that public attention will drift towards more immediate and solvable public issues.

Komen Foundation—Constraining Political Involvement

In 2012, the Susan G. Komen Foundation suffered a highly publicized backlash against what appeared to be the politicization of its distribution of donated funds. One of the largest and most well-known breast cancer nonprofit organizations in the world, the Susan G. Komen foundation raises hundreds of millions USD per year from contributions and fundraising events; foundation funds are then spent on breast cancer research, as well as preventative efforts such as screenings and education. In late January 2012, the Komen Foundation announced that it would no longer provide grants for breast cancer screenings to women's health organization Planned Parenthood Federation of America.

The Komen Foundation's termination of this funding relationship (which began in 2007) was explained as resulting from an internal change in funding eligibility rules, which would exclude organizations being investigated by Congress. At the time of this rule change, Planned Parenthood was being investigated by the U.S. House of Representatives to ensure the organization's compliance with guidelines prohibiting the use of Federal funds for abortion services.

Announcement of the cessation of funding was met with widespread negativity among Planned Parenthood supporters and leadership. Planned Parenthood President Cecile Richards immediately depicted Komen's policy change, as well as the investigation by Congress, as being motivated by pro-life political interests. Describing this decision as "hurtful," Richards stated "It's hard to understand how an organization with whom we share a mission of saving women's lives could have bowed to this kind of bullying,"[13]

While pro-life groups applauded the Komen Foundation, the far greater bulk of public reactivity was in support of Planned Parenthood. Within 24 hours of the Komen announcement, Planned Parenthood had received over 6,000 individual donations—a highly significant increase over the average rate of less than two hundred donations per day.[14] By the end of the same week, the Komen Foundation clarified its policy to exclude only those organizations under criminal investigations, effectively restoring funding to Planned Parenthood.[15]

The Komen example illustrates both the role of the intermediate public and the significance of symbolic capital in constraint efforts. Through its organizing and promotional efforts, the Komen Foundation had successfully built a large base of supporters, donors, and activists with a shared interest in breast cancer; the solidarity of Komen supporters (sometimes referred to as the "pink army") as well as the overall reputation of the organization was due in no small part to its focused and non-controversial mission of finding a cure for breast cancer.[16] As constructed by the Komen Foundation, the fight against breast cancer transcends all ages, races, and political views, thus requiring all women (and the men who love them) to become proactively involved. Under this narrative, the Komen Foundation was able to amass a substantial quantity of symbolic power, becoming the dominant organization in relation to breast cancer, as well as women's health more broadly.

The announcement of the defunding of Planned Parenthood thus represented a severe fracture of the symbolic basis of existing relationships with its partner organizations and supporter base through the prioritization of political views over women's health. Despite the policy reversal and the resignation of Vice President for Public Policy, Karen Handel, the Komen Foundation had lost much of the faith of its supporters. This loss of symbolic capital led to significant decreases in donations; disclosures for FY2012 reported a 22% decline in income over the previous year.[17] Similarly, participation in Komen's "Race for the Cure" fundraising events declined by 19% during the second half of 2012.[18]

Steam Workshop—Successful Constraint in the Entertainment Industry

In April 2015, American video game development firm Valve Corporation experienced a massive backlash from its customers after making changes to its popular game distribution platform Steam. Citing extremely intense criticism from its user base, Valve reversed these changes after less than one week. Central to understanding this example is the development of the relationship between the user-oriented nature of the community and the more conventional commercial nature of Valve itself.

Valve Corporation began developing and publishing video games for personal computers and game consoles in the late 1990s. As broadband internet became more widely available throughout the United States, many firms within the broader entertainment industry (e.g. gaming, music, software) began developing online platforms to deliver content to users. In 2003, Valve launched its online platform, Steam, with limited functionality; users who purchased physical copies of Valve games could use Steam to apply updates (i.e. patches) to their games, to play online against other users, or to download additional content.

Such online platforms were not, however, being developed solely for the benefit of users. As the availability and speed of internet access increased, preventing lost revenue from software piracy (especially through file sharing over peer-to-peer networks) became a priority throughout the entertainment industry. Specifically citing piracy concerns, Valve began *requiring* the use of the Steam platform to validate the installation of its 2004 game, *Half-Life 2*.[19]

The functionality of the Steam platform was further expanded by allowing customers to purchase and utilize *digital* copies of games, rather than conventional *physical* copies.[20] While such digital distribution systems may be more convenient for users, they also raise significant questions regarding rights of ownership. Under the "First Sale Doctrine," consumers possess limited rights over the physical copies of copyrighted works (e.g. books, video games) they have legitimately purchased; reselling or trading a physical copy is protected, but actions which violate the rights of the copyright holder (e.g. duplication) are not.

Based on these considerations, Steam (and other such digital distribution platforms) seem to be contrary to the interests of consumers: without physical copies of games, consumers lose their capacity to sell or trade games they dislike or grow tired of, and digital rights management (DRM) systems introduce seemingly unnecessary hassles.[21] Valve's 2004 decision to begin making Steam mandatory for users would thus appear to be an effort to protect its economic capital at the cost of a marginal reduction of its symbolic capital—manifest in this context as reputation among video game enthusiasts.

However, rather than simply use Steam as a mechanism for extracting profits, Valve continued to add features based on the perceived and expressed wishes of its user community. The quantity and variety of games available on Steam rapidly increased through publishing agreements with third-party and independent game developers, continuously attracting more users.[22] Social networking functions and online multiplayer options were added to Steam, increasingly making games an interpersonal and immersive experience.[23] The community-oriented perception of Steam was effectively solidified with the 2011 introduction of the Steam Workshop, which Valve described as "a central hub of player-created content and tools to publish, organize, and download that content into your games."[24] Through Steam Workshop, individuals could create various modifications (i.e. mods) to Workshop-enabled games and share them with other players on Steam; mods ranged in complexity from adjustments in graphics (e.g. the color and texture of water) to the addition of entirely new quests or objectives.

Modding proved to be extremely popular among Steam users, creating both economic and cultural/symbolic connections between Valve and the Steam user community. For most games, mods and modding tools were offered to game owners through Steam at no additional cost. Steam Workshop thus generated a mutually beneficial economic relationship; users benefited by extending the replay value of previously purchased games, while Valve enjoyed an ever increasing share of the gaming market and a highly loyal user base. Perhaps more importantly, the creation of a free (and minimally regulated or limited) marketplace for mods signified an authentic connection to the user community by tapping directly into what Lessig termed "R/W culture." By refusing to place limits on the creativity of the user community and denying the use of mods as a mechanism for extracting additional profits, Steam Workshop represented an intense symbolic relationship between Valve and their users—one which has effectively served to legitimize Valve's dominance of the digital gaming market.[25]

This symbolic relationship, however, was temporarily strained in 2015, with the announcement that Valve would integrate a payment system to the Steam Workshop, beginning with Bethesda Software's highly popular game, *Elder Scrolls V: Skyrim*. Creators of mods would have the ability to sell their modifications, or continue to offer them for free; specific prices for mods would be set by developers, with revenues divided between the mod developers, Valve, and Bethesda (the owner of *Skyrim*'s intellectual properties). Both Bethesda and Valve presented this change as a means of improving the user community. Bethesda's announcement specifically invoked a desire for increased fairness to mod creators:

> We believe mod developers are just that: developers... We believe most mods should be free. But we also believe our community wants to reward the very best creators, and that they deserve to be rewarded. We believe the best should be paid for their work and treated like the game developers they are. But again, we don't think it's right for us to decide who those creators are or what they create.[26]

Valve's announcement contained similar remarks, suggesting that the insertion of market forces would create long-term benefits for the Steam community.

> If you've been using the Steam Workshop, you already know how much incredible content is available for many of your favorite games. By paying for mods and supporting the people that made them, you enable those artists and creators to continue working on their mods and inspire new modders to try their hand in creating new, higher quality items and experiences.[27]

This apparent intent to replace the internal logic of the Steam community with market logic was underscored by remarks made by Valve CEO Gabe Newell; seemingly channeling Friedrich Hayek, Newell defended this policy change by exhorting Steam users to "Think of money as information."[28]

Skyrim fans (as well as the broader Steam community), however, reacted to these changes in a negative and highly vocal manner. Across a variety of social networking and gaming-oriented news sites, Steam users debated the various problems posed by the paid mod system; in less than 24 hours after the announced changes, 34,000 users signed a petition created on change.org calling for Valve to remove the paid content option.[29]

Steam users expressed a range of objections to the paid mod system, many of which contained some suggestion of inconsistency between it and the norms of the community. In particular, the market logic of the paid mod system was perceived as a violation of the logic of sharing and reciprocity that had emerged within the modding community. The change.org petition against Valve, while not necessarily comprising all such objections, nonetheless serves as a fairly representative example of such sentiments:

> The workshop is a place for people to share content with each other they made so all can enjoy it for free... Mods should be a free creation. Creations made by people who wish to add to the game so others can also enjoy said creation with the game.[30]

Creativity and sharing, however, were not the only basis for concerns; issues of authorship, economic fairness, and consumer protection were raised as well.

As the modding community had been operating on a principle of "share and share alike," authorship of mods was of minimal consequence; creators of mods regularly borrowed from or built upon the works of other mod creators, with only the normative caveat that such borrowing should be acknowledged. The introduction of payment, however, created crises regarding authorship, as a lack of acknowledgment was transformed from a social *faux pas* to a form of economic exploitation. Perhaps ironically, the first paid mod to be introduced for *Skyrim* was taken down, after complaints that it utilized components from the works of other mod creators without their permission.[31] Rather than be subject to such misappropriation, numerous mod creators opted to remove their works from the Steam Workshop entirely.[32] Users expressed additional concerns from a consumer standpoint. Purchasers of mods would have a reasonable expectation of future product support from mod creators; however, no mechanisms existed to ensure that mod sellers would behave in such responsive or responsible manners.

The intensity of such negative reactions was readily noticed by executives at Valve and Bethesda; the removal of the paid mod system was announced on April 27, just four days after its introduction. In statements regarding this abrupt change of policy, executives validated the concerns of angry users and reiterated their good intentions regarding improvements to the Steam community. Valve User Interaction Designer Alden Kroll explains this occurrence as a poor execution of a good idea:

> [W]e underestimated the differences between our previously successful revenue sharing models, and the addition of paid mods to Skyrim's workshop. We understand our own game's communities pretty well, but stepping into an established, years old modding community in Skyrim was probably not the right place to start iterating. We think this made us miss the mark pretty badly, even though we believe there's a useful feature somewhere here.[33]

Slightly before announcing the decision to cancel the paid mods option, Valve co-founder Gabe Newell attempted to dispel the perception that this was an attempt at increasing profits:

> Let's assume for a second that we are stupidly greedy. So far the paid mods have generated $10K total. That's like 1% of the cost of the incremental email the program has generated for Valve employees (yes, I mean pissing off the Internet costs you a million bucks in just a couple of days). That's not stupidly greedy, that's stupidly stupid.[34]

The Steam Workshop example can thus be understood as a successful effort of elite constraint, utilizing social and economic mechanisms. While there is insufficient data to assess the effect of this effort on Valve's economic capital, the content and intensity of comments by Steam users suggests a significant threat to Valve's symbolic capital.[35]

Insularity and Repression

As explained in Chapter 3, new communications technologies have opened up an intermediate space within the public sphere, wherein non-elite actors (i.e. politically interested and motivated members of the general public) can, to a limited degree, constitute themselves as groups and engage in symbolically productive communicative activities. Furthermore, new communications technologies have enabled emergent cultural practices based on information sharing and collaborative labor (i.e. Lessig's R/W culture). While such changes have led to neither the elimination of dominant layers within societies, nor to the wholesale displacement of actors within the dominant layer, they have nonetheless altered the relationships between dominant and non-dominant layers by changing the dynamics of elite constraint; more specifically, by increasing the effectiveness and practicability of social mechanisms of constraint.

Unsurprisingly, such changes have not gone unnoticed by elite actors across nearly all types of polities. While social constraint may simply become a part of the normal flux of elite competition, creating advantages for some and disadvantages for others, it may also serve to weaken broader elite/non-elite divisions. That the conservation of symbolic capital and the maintenance of the symbolic ordering of the social whole are mandatory aims for actors within the field of dominance cannot be overstated. As such, efforts to restructure contexts of forms of communication may be better understood as efforts to reduce the practicability and/or effectiveness of social mechanisms of constraint. Through various means, elite actors may attempt to *insulate* themselves from negative public reactions by making certain constraint efforts riskier or more difficult. Such efforts at insularity are not oriented at increasing individual stores of symbolic capital, but rather at preserving the larger symbolic order by negating the public's capacity to negate symbolic power.

Privacy and Chilling Effects in Online Communication

One highly significant means of decreasing the practicability of constraint efforts, particularly those involving social and/or physical mechanisms is through surveillance of online communications. While surveillance of private communications may be reasonably assumed to exist within authoritarian or partially democratic states, the revelation of the existence of widespread surveillance programs in major democratic states (e.g. the United States, France, Germany, the United Kingdom) in 2013 was fairly shocking. Awareness of various programs for the bulk collection of electronic communications and communications records (i.e. metadata) by the

U.S. National Security Agency (NSA), Britain's Government Communications Headquarters (GCHQ), among others, has prompted renewed discussions of the importance of privacy and freedoms of communication and inquiry.

Surveillance of online communications is commonly discussed as creating risks of chilling effects in the context of speech and opinion-formation. As initially utilized by the U.S. Supreme Court in the 1950s, "chilling effects" refers to the tendency of overly broad legislation to stifle an individual's internalized sense of propriety in the free exploration of ideas and associations.[36] According to Associate Justice Felix Frankfurter, the various protections offered by the First and Fourteenth Amendments to the U.S. Constitution signify the importance of a "free play of the spirit" in regard to open-minded inquiry and communication. Government actions which serve to inhibit this free mindedness create harms both for the affected individuals and the overall health of the polity, even if those actions do not specifically prohibit constitutionally protected individual activities.[37]

In the context of elite constraint and surveillance of online communication, the concerns of chilling effects are fairly straightforward: the presence of surveillance of communication may inhibit individual willingness to discuss controversial issues or explore unorthodox ideas. Recent survey research among Americans suggests that such chilling effects are, in fact, quite real. A 2014 study by the Pew Research Center found that while 86% of respondents would discuss NSA surveillance issues in face-to-face conversations, only 42% of respondents who use Facebook or Twitter would have such conversations using these online platforms.[38] Perhaps even more pernicious is the fear of coercion, discrimination, or other forms of harm arising from information collected through surveillance. Top-secret documents leaked to journalists by NSA whistleblower Edward Snowden describe NSA strategies to discredit individuals advocating "radical" political ideals by using information gathered through surveillance to identify their "vulnerabilities of character or credibility."[39]

The potential for surveillance of online communications and activities to stifle expression and create an environment of fear and suspicion is not limited, however, to dissidents and radicals within the political realm. Surveillance of the social media activities of employees has become a routine responsibility for human resources personnel. The practice of monitoring the online activities of employees has become so pervasive as to prompt government action to restore employee privacy. In a number of rulings since 2012, the U.S. National Labor Relations Board has held that while such monitoring is permissible, employment contracts and policies cannot abridge the rights of employees to discuss wages and working conditions with third parties through social media.[40] Employers can, however, sanction employees for using social media to disclose personal or otherwise protected information about other employees.[41] A similar practice involves employers requiring the disclosure of usernames and passwords to social media sites for both current employees and job applicants; as of 2015, this practice was specifically prohibited in 21 states.[42]

Regardless of the source (i.e. government or business), surveillance creates a disparity of power, in which the object of surveillance is necessarily imbued with a decreased capacity for autonomous behavior.[43] The impact of surveillance on the practicability of mechanisms of constraint, particularly social constraint is clear; the exploration and communication of controversial or unconventional ideas and issue positions carries not only the potential for social stigma, but also for retribution by governmental or economic institutions.

The Declining Significance of Authority

As discussed in Chapter 3, mechanisms of communicative-productive activity within intermediate public spaces are not completely independent from the same activities at the elite level; communicative production at the intermediate level is nearly always generated in reaction to elite level productions (i.e. statements by elite actors). As such, the structures of the intermediate public are seemingly ideally suited for social mechanisms of constraint, as a great deal of the activities of the intermediate public are oriented towards weakening the authority of actors at the elite level. As previously mentioned, authority entails some pretense of epistemic superiority on behalf of the elite actor; such a pretense, however, is unsustainable in the presence of both the technological capacity to find information on nearly anything, and the cultural disposition towards uninhibited flows of information.

Within this context, the intricacies of issues of collective interest become *knowable* to any individual, despite not necessarily *being known* by them. Authority's access to specialized knowledge creates an aura of mystery which supports the epistemic gap; to the extent that the gap between positions appears bridgeable, authority becomes demystified and thus less deserving of special communicative privilege.[44] As the distinction between the authority and non-authority positions is reduced, the agency of the non-authority is increased, and the choice of simply rejecting the presence of authority relative to a certain topic is viable.[45]

Oppositional action—the challenging and ultimately rejecting of authority of elite public actors—thus serves an important function in that it represents a more active and sophisticated form of withdrawal of acclamation, one that may improve the functioning of opinion-formation processes overall. As identified in Chapter 1, one problematic aspect of Habermas' concept of the "reflexive public" was that the ideal public must carefully monitor the actions and statements of elite public actors, yet the public only possesses a weak capacity to act or produce feedback on such evaluations. It is taken on faith that the internal processes of the journalistic profession will sufficiently monitor and "police" elite public actors, insuring quality outputs. Oppositional action from the intermediate public, however, provides a direct mechanism for "policing" elite level outputs; both the spirit and function of oppositional action are perfectly encapsulated in political blogger (and current managing editor of Wonkette.com) Ken Layne's famous rebuke of journalist Robert Fisk: "We can fact check your ass."[46] Thus, actions of the intermediate public can serve as a "social mechanism of control" by calling out improper behaviors of elite actors or unacceptable outputs from the elite level.

The question remains, however, as to the net effect of such oppositional activity at the intermediate level. On the one hand, such oppositional action should be valorized, as it serves to help hold elite public actors accountable to the public interest—to "keep their feet to the fire," so to speak. In alternative terminology, to the extent that co-respective behaviors are exhibited by public actors at the elite level, oppositional action from the intermediate public serves to disrupt such insularity from the outside. In this regard, the capacity for the intermediate public to "stir the pot" through oppositional communicative activity stimulates existing processes of elite competition.

Opposition, however, comes at a hidden cost. Beyond the specific monitoring of elite-level outputs, oppositional actions signify a kind of cultural rejection of epistemic privilege; in this context, the potential power of authority diminishes. As the relative capacity for any public actor or institution to hold authority decreases, the relative weight of visibility in the formation of influence increases. Unlike authority, which emerges from the relationship with the public at large, visibility can be acquired without such public assent; through mechanisms of public relations and advertisement, or through ownership of media firms, economic capital can be directly converted into visibility. This changes the nature of competition at the elite level by rendering public actors without positional connections to resourceful communicative entities less able to compete for influence.

Furthermore, it is questionable as to whether or not oppositional action creates "better" elite level outputs. While such a form of social constraint may be capable of targeting inconsistent or inaccurate elite outputs on a case-by-case basis, it is not necessarily capable of establishing alternative discourse norms at the elite level. The net effect of social constraint emerging from the intermediate public on the public elite is thus ambiguous. To the extent that oppositional actions disrupt any exclusion or insularity at the elite level, openness and competition in public communication are enhanced, as is the accountability of elites. In situations where the elites in question claim their authority based on expert knowledge, challenges by the public can lead to a more shared distribution of knowledge, and open up new topics for public discussion.[47]

However, oppositional actions undermine not just the authority of elite actors, but the very function of authority itself; in so doing, gaining the public's recognition (as a valid holder of authority) risks becoming a strategically useless action in the competition for influence. As hyper-scrutiny from the intermediate public becomes an increasingly common aspect of the competitive environment in which elite actors operate, elite actors may simply abandon any pretense of authority and construct their legitimacy on other grounds.

The 2009 Iranian Election—Violence and Repression in the Networked Public

The domestic and international protests following the presidential elections held in the Islamic Republic of Iran in June 2009 represent an interesting study of the communicative-productive capacity of the intermediate public. In addition to the usage of social media for political activism, the Iran case is notable for the level of involvement of individuals outside Iran with seemingly no immediate connection to the outcome of the election.

The campaign phase of the 2009 Iranian election exhibited widespread usage of networked communications by both the incumbent President Mahmoud Ahmadinejad and the lead challenger Mir-Hossein Mousavi. Faced with strict limitations on usage of state-run media outlets, Mousavi supporters and campaign strategists turned to networked communications, specifically social networking sites such as Facebook, to build their support base and mobilize anti-incumbent sentiments.[48] The importance of online presence for strengthening political support was not overlooked by conservatives, however; via Facebook and his personal blog (www.ahmadinejad.ir/), Pres. Ahmadinejad worked to cultivate a following among (mostly young) conservative Muslims throughout the Middle East.[49] Such multimedia and multiplatform campaign strategies are estimated to have driven the costs of both the Mousavi and Ahmadinejad campaigns into the range of $30–40 Million USD—substantially higher than previous election cycles.[50]

This reliance on networked communications, however, became a liability for Mousavi supporters. Roughly two weeks before the election, access to Facebook was temporarily blocked by the Iranian intelligence ministry.[51] Despite President Ahmadinejad's denial of any knowledge or political involvement in the decision, the blockage is suspected to have been an attempt to frustrate Mousavi supporters.[52] Far more brazen manipulation of internet availability by the Iranian government occurred immediately prior to the June 12th election. Within the week prior to the election, the volume of text message service (SMS) usage jumped from roughly 55 million messages per day to 110 million daily messages.[53] Shortly before midnight on the evening before polls opened, the SMS system of Iran's primary mobile carrier went down, substantially impairing pro-reform groups from monitoring polling results independently of state-controlled media sources.[54] While this is generally suspected to have been the result of intentional action by the Iranian government, it is possible that the massive increases in network traffic contributed to overall system instability.[55]

Such direct manipulation of the telecom infrastructure in Iran expanded as news of polling results showing a wide margin of victory of Ahmadinejad turned into claims of electoral fraud.[56] On Saturday, June 13th, the SMS shutdown was expanded to include all mobile phone service, and access to multiple internet sites (including both social networking and pro-reform sites) was blocked.[57] Iranian authorities also employed less sophisticated techniques by jamming broadcast signals from BBC Persian TV.[58] Given the locked down state of the telecom infrastructure in Iran and the limitations placed on journalistic activities, one of the main actions undertaken by protest groups was to document and distribute both the intensity of the contestation of the election results and the severity of the governmental reactions via SMS messaging and distribution of video clips.

Micro-blogging website Twitter was one of the most visible nexuses of online activity to promote awareness of the election aftermath. Likely due to the ease of posting messages via SMS and the ability to easily redistribute and search messages, Twitter was considered the primary source for distribution of ground-level information, coordination of protest activities (online and offline), as well as criticisms of media coverage.[59] The importance of Twitter for the Iranian protestors did not go unnoticed. Beta versions of Farsi language tools were added to Twitter (as well as Google) to enable more Iranians to utilize the service.[60] Additionally, the U.S. State Department requested that Twitter administrators postpone scheduled system maintenance so that the service would not be down during Iranian peak usage times.[61]

Not surprisingly, within a relatively short period of time, Twitter became an increasingly chaotic information environment, plagued by high numbers of repostings and suspicion of counter-intelligence efforts by the Iranian government. One of the most widely circulated guides for Twitter-based strategies for following and participating in the Iranian protest movement provided the following suggestions for optimal usage of the service for organization of information and security of Iranians:

> 2. Hashtags, the only two legitimate hashtags being used by bloggers in Iran are #iranelection and #gr88, other hashtag ideas run the risk of diluting the conversation.
>
> 3. Keep you bull$hit filter up! Security forces are now setting up twitter accounts to spread disinformation by posing as Iranian protesters. Please don't retweet impetuously, try to confirm information with reliable sources before retweeting. The legitimate sources are not hard to find and follow.
>
> 4. Help cover the bloggers: change your twitter settings so that your location is TEHRAN and your time zone is GMT +3.30. Security forces are hunting for bloggers using location and timezone searches. If we all become "Iranians" it becomes much harder to find them.

5. Don't blow their cover! If you discover a genuine source, please don't publicize their name or location on a website. These bloggers are in REAL danger. Spread the word discretely through your own networks but don't signpost them to the security forces. People are dying there, for real, please keep that in mind.[62]

Despite the efforts of the Iranian government, video clips of violence against protestors were widely circulated through video sharing sites (e.g. YouTube, Google Video) as well.[63] One of the most widely distributed video clips documented the fatal shooting of protest observer Neda Agha-Soltan by a militia volunteer, quickly making her a rallying figure for the protest movement.[64]

Beyond helping to increase international awareness of the grievances of the Iranian people, networked communications were used to provide technical support from users outside Iran; specifically, a variety of groups in the United States and Europe provided tools to allow Iranians secure and anonymous internet communications. One prominent Western resource for cyber protest activities which emerged was NedaNet.org, named after slain protest observer Neda Soltan. The organizers of NedaNet described their objectives and motivations as follows:

> This is the resource page for NedaNet, a network of hackers formed to support the democratic revolution in Iran. Our mission is to help the Iranian people by setting up networks of proxy servers, anonymizers, and any other appropriate technologies that can enable them to communicate and organize—a network beyond the censorship or control of the Iranian regime.
>
> NedaNet doesn't have leaders or a manifesto or even much in the way of organization. We're not affiliated with any nation or religion. We're just computer hackers and computer users from all over the planet doing what we can to help the Iranian people in their struggle for freedom.
>
> NedaNet does have contacts on the ground in Iran. We are actively and directly cooperating with the revolutionaries (though for obvious security reasons most of us don't know who the contacts are). By helping us, you can help them.[65]

In addition to such ICT usage to increase international awareness of the ground-level situation in Iran, a number of Iranian governmental websites were targets of cyberattacks as part of the protest against the Presidential election. The primary form of attack utilized in this (and similar cases) is the denial-of-service (DoS) attack in which the target website (e.g. www.president.ir—the official website of the Iranian Presidency) is flooded with excessive information requests, effectively overloading the capacity of the server(s) on which the website is hosted.[66] Such attacks may originate from a single source or from multiple sources, in which case, it would be considered a distributed-denial-of-service (DDoS) attack.

Many of the sites and guides offering instructions on more basic forms of support for Iranian protesters contained additional information on DDoS attacks and targets.[67] The "#iranelection beginners guide to cyberwar" listed recommended forms of ICT usage at multiple levels of engagement, the highest of which—"cyberwarrior"—provided strategies for engaging in DDoS attacks with minor caveats:

> All I will say is that you must only risk hardware you can afford to lose as you face the distinct possibility of attracting a robust counter-attack. Also please only engage in surgical DOS strikes against targets that are specifically designated by trusted Iranians, and only during the designated windows of time.[68]

Endorsement of DDoS attacks came from more prominent websites as well; on June 14th, Daily KOS hosted a blog entry plainly titled "How to Take Down an Iranian Government Website" which contained links to software tools and specific governmental websites to target.[69] Not long after, however, a number of additional entries arose opposing such tactics, arguing that the network traffic produced by DDoS attacks decreased the capacity of internet users inside Iran to get messages and video out of the country.[70]

Within a relatively short period of time, opposition to the usage of DDoS attacks became more prominent than their support, based partially on normative grounds and primarily on practical considerations regarding the amount of stress the Iranian infrastructure was capable of sustaining. One frequently accessed blog entry by technology scholar Evgeny Morovoz neatly describes the situation thus:

> Some wise folks have been cautioning against participating in DDOS attacks, for they are only likely to slow down Internet in Iran for everyone, not just Ahmadinejad's supporters… But these little subtleties get lost on an angry online mob that wants revengue on Ahmadinejad without taking the effort to educate themselves about the repercussions of their cyber-activity. It's a shame that some American bloggers are participating in this campaign and are even encouraging others to take up their "cyber-arms". Not only is this irresponsible and probably illegal, it also hurts users in Iran and gives their hard-line government another reason to suspect "foreign intervention"—albeit via computer networks—into Iranian politics.[71]

The Iranian example raises particularly interesting questions regarding the legitimate boundaries of the usage of networked communications. On the one hand, the structures of the intermediate public allow for the rapid emergence and mobilization of communities of shared interests; on the other hand, actions undertaken through the structures of the intermediate public space lack any immediate manifestation of physical consequences. As the effects of cyberattacks or other, more aggressive online activities, were distant or non-existent for persons living outside Iran, the DDoS attacks appear more as acts of nihilism than political action.

With this in mind, the potential problem with using cyberattacks as a form of protest becomes apparent. The problem is not, per se, that in attacking various Iranian servers, freedom of communication is being denied to the Iranian government; as the observed behaviors explained in the previous section suggest, the Iranian regime has little interest in upholding such a freedom. Rather, the problem appears to be that through cyberattacks, the usage of networked communication as a weapon, or more accurately, as a mechanism of domination, is legitimized. To the extent that networked communications are used as means of attacking the state, the Iranian regime's use of networked communications for the exercise of state power becomes symbolically legitimized.

Conclusion

Through the communicative-productive capacity of the intermediate public, like-minded individuals have an increased ability to express their grievances and attempt to constrain elite behaviors. However, as illustrated through the examples in this chapter, successful constraint occurs within fairly limited circumstances. Successful constraint requires a clear and consistent demand which articulates what is wrong, and how it can be made right. Similarly, this demand for a correction must be actually achievable—preferably narrowed to discrete actions that can be taken or decisions that can be reversed. With this in mind, the generalization can be made that elites in certain positions are more capable of reacting to constraint than others; specifically, elite actors and firms in business fields are more likely to be able to reverse unpopular decisions than political elites operating within more bureaucratic structures.

Successful constraint also appears to require an authentic and commonly held sense of the symbolic relationship between elite actors and their communities; claims that elites have failed to follow the shared interests and commitments underlying such symbolic relationships are extremely powerful, but only to the extent that such interests and commitments are meaningful to constituencies, users, supporters, etc.

Given the relatively narrow opportunities for constraint, actors and outputs of the intermediate public may instead become integrated into existing issue camps or elite institutions; such integration into normal competitive processes may lead to significant political changes, but they are unlikely to fundamentally interfere with the functioning of the elite realm. Political changes (perhaps even significant ones) do occur, but they do so as the result of the elite realm's internal competitive processes, rather than through the external disruption of a constraint effort. From the perspective of non-elite actors, normalization and integration represent a trade-off. On the one hand, communicative production in the intermediate public becomes another means for citizens to have their voice heard within the competitive-pluralist political system; on the other hand, the potential power of the demos as articulated through intermediate public structures ceases to be self-organizing.

Notes

1 Margolis and Resnick, *Politics as Usual: The Cyberspace "Revolution,"* 208.
2 Ibid., 2.
3 Bourdieu, *Language and Symbolic Power*, 202.
4 Sternbergh, "The Spreadsheet Psychic."
5 Stelter, "Times to Host Blog on Politics and Polls."
6 Hayes, "What Will Nate Silver Do Next?"
7 "Annotated Captions of KONY 2012 in English | Dotsub."
8 Wasserman, "'KONY 2012' Tops 100 Million Views, Becomes the Most Viral Video in History."
9 "In New Video on Eve of Kony 2012 Day of Action, Senators Underscore Support for U.S. Efforts to Help Capture Joseph Kony| News Releases| U.S. Senator Chris Coons of Delaware."
10 "Senate Condemns Crimes of Joseph Kony and Lord's Resistance Army| News Releases| U.S. Senator Chris Coons of Delaware."
11 Carroll, "Kony 2012 Cover the Night Fails to Move from the Internet to the Streets."
12 "Overspending and Decline in Funding Force Invisible Children to Announce 2015 Closure."
13 "Cancer Charity Halts Grants to Planned Parenthood | Fox News."
14 Kliff and Sun, "Planned Parenthood Says Komen Decision Causes Donation Spike."
15 Preston and Harris, "Komen Reverses Stance on Planned Parenthood Grants."
16 Magazine, "Komen and Planned Parenthood."
17 Hiltzik, "Susan G. Komen Foundation Discovers the Price of Playing Politics."
18 Wallis, "Komen Foundation Works to Regain Support After Planned Parenthood Controversy."
19 "Gamers Get Playing Half-Life 2."
20 "A Brief History of Steam."
21 Plunkett, "Steam Is 10 Today. Remember When It Sucked?"
22 "Steam Surpasses 13 Million Accounts." "Eidos launching with Steam."
23 "Steam Community Features Launch | The Escapist." Kuchera, "Valve launches Steam Community, perhaps a bit soon | Ars Technica."
24 "About Steam Workshop."
25 While exact sales figures are not available, many estimates place Valve's share of the downloaded games market near 70%. Chiang, "The Master of Online Mayhem."
26 "Skyrim Mods."
27 "Steam Workshop Now Supporting Paid Creations."
28 Hayek, "The Use of Knowledge in Society."
29 Chalk, "Petition against paid mods on Steam draws 34,000 signatures in a day—PC Gamer."
30 "Valve."
31 Parlock, "The first paid Skyrim mod has been pulled."
32 Tassi, "Valve's Paid 'Skyrim' Mods Are a Legal, Ethical and Creative Disaster."

33 Kroll, "Removing Payment."
34 "MODs and Steam • /r/gaming."
35 As a privately held corporation, Valve has minimal obligations for the disclosure of financial information (including sales revenues) under U.S. law at the time of writing.
36 "Wieman v. Updegraff 344 U.S. 183 (1952)."
37 Kaminski and Witnov, "The Conforming Effect."
38 Hampton et al., "Social Media and the 'Spiral of Silence.'"
39 "Top-Secret Document Reveals NSA Spied on Porn Habits as Part of Plan to Discredit 'Radicalizers.'"
40 "NLRB Continues Aggressive Crackdown on Social Media Policies."
41 "NLRB Signs Off on Employer Social Media Policy as Legal."
42 "Will Employers Still Ask for Facebook Passwords in 2014?" "State Laws About Social Media Privacy."
43 Richards, "Dangers of Surveillance, The."
44 Sennett, *Authority*, 158–9.
45 Flathman, *The Practice of Political Authority: Authority and the Authoritative*, 192.
46 "Kenlayne.com (Internet Archive: Dec 14, 2001)."
47 Bohman, "Citizenship and Norms of Publicity: Wide Public Reason in Cosmopolitan Societies," 192.
48 Bozorgmehr, "Facebook Sets Tone in Iran's Electoral Contest."
49 Setrakian, "Iran's Pres. Candidates Recognize the Web as a Go-To to Win."
50 Peskin, "Iranian Election Costs Millions."
51 Ribeiro, "Facebook Blocked in Iran Ahead of Elections."
52 Sayah, "Ahmadinejad Denies Calling for Facebook Ban."
53 "Election SMS Fever Running High in Iran." "SMS Messages Rise to 110 Million a Day amid Presidential Campaigns."
54 Faris and Heacock, "Cracking Down on Digital Communication and Political Organizing in Iran." "Massive Censorship Accompanies Ahmadinejad 'Victory.'"
55 Cowie, "A Closer Look at Iran's State of Internet, Strange Transit Changes in Wake of Controversial Election."
56 "Election Officials: Ahmadinejad Has Large Lead in Iran."
57 "Mousavi Officially Contests Iran Election Results."
58 "Iran Blocks TV, Radio and Phones—but Web Proves More Difficult."
59 Terdiman, "'#CNNFAIL': Twitterverse Slams Network's Iran Absence"; "A Twitter Timeline of the Iran Election."
60 Kiss, "Google and Facebook Roll out Farsi Language Tools."
61 Grossman, "Iran's Protests: Why Twitter Is the Medium of the Movement."
62 Reinikainen, "#iranelection Cyberwar Guide for Beginners."
63 Sweney, "Google Chief: Iran Can't Control the Net."
64 "Iran Doctor Tells of Neda's Death."
65 Raymond, "NedaNet Resource Page."
66 "How a 'Denial of Service' Attack Works."
67 Shachtman, "Activists Launch Hack Attacks on Tehran Regime."
68 Reinikainen, "#iranelection – Part 2 – Cyberwar Guide for Beginners."
69 "How to Take Down an Iranian Government Website."
70 "Do NOT DDOS Iranian Websites."
71 Morozov, "DDOS Attacks on Iran's Web-Sites: What a Stupid Idea!"

References

"About Steam Workshop." Accessed July 28, 2015. http://steamcommunity.com/workshop/workshopsubmitinfo/.

"A Brief History of Steam." *Maximum PC*, April 27, 2015. www.maximumpc.com//brief-history-steam-2015/.

"Annotated Captions of KONY 2012 in English | Dotsub." Accessed August 15, 2015. https://dotsub.com/view/ef3d7b6c-eab5-478a-a51c-d27166d27dcc/viewTranscript/eng.

"A Twitter Timeline of the Iran Election," June 26, 2009. www.newsweek.com/id/203953.

Bohman, J. "Citizenship and Norms of Publicity: Wide Public Reason in Cosmopolitan Societies." *Political Theory* 27, no. 2 (April1999): 176–202. doi: 10.1177/0090591799027002002.

Bourdieu, Pierre. *Language and Symbolic Power*. Cambridge: Polity Press, 1991.

Bozorgmehr, Najmeh. "Facebook Sets Tone in Iran's Electoral Contest." *Financial Times*, May 13, 2009. www.ft.com/cms/s/0/9a232204-3f57-11de-ae4f-00144feabdc0.html?nclick_check=1.

"Cancer Charity Halts Grants to Planned Parenthood | Fox News." Accessed August 17, 2015. www.foxnews.com/us/2012/01/31/cancer-charity-halts-grants-to-planned-parenthood-1227146736/.

Carroll, Rory. "Kony 2012 Cover the Night Fails to Move from the Internet to the Streets." *The Guardian*, April 21, 2012, sec. World news. www.theguardian.com/world/2012/apr/21/kony-2012-campaign-uganda-warlord.

Chalk, Andy. "Petition against paid mods on Steam draws 34,000 signatures in a day – PC Gamer," April 23, 2015. www.pcgamer.com/petition-against-paid-mods-on-steam-draws-34000-signatures-in-a-day/.

Chiang, Oliver. "The Master of Online Mayhem." *Forbes*, February 9, 2011. www.forbes.com/forbes/2011/0228/technology-gabe-newell-videogames-valve-online-mayhem.html.

Cowie, Jim. "A Closer Look at Iran's State of Internet, Strange Transit Changes in Wake of Controversial Election," June 14, 2009. www.circleid.com/posts/20090614_closer_look_at_iran_internet_strange_changes/.

"Do NOT DDOS Iranian Websites," June 15, 2009. www.dailykos.com/story/2009/6/15/742591/-Do-NOT-DDOS-Iranian-websites.

"Eidos launching with Steam," March 15, 2007. www.valvesoftware.com/news/?id=986.

"Election Officials: Ahmadinejad Has Large Lead in Iran," June 12, 2009. www.cnn.com/2009/WORLD/meast/06/12/iran.election/index.html.

"Election SMS Fever Running High in Iran," June 11, 2009. www.presstv.ir/detail.aspx?id=97772§ionid=3510212.

Faris, Rob, and Rebekah Heacock. "Cracking Down on Digital Communication and Political Organizing in Iran," June 15, 2009. http://opennet.net/blog/2009/06/cracking-down-digital-communication-and-political-organizing-iran.

Flathman, Richard E. *The Practice of Political Authority: Authority and the Authoritative*. Chicago, IL: University of Chicago Press, 1980.

"Gamers Get Playing Half-Life 2," November 17, 2004. http://newsvote.bbc.co.uk/mpapps/pagetools/print/news.bbc.co.uk/2/hi/technology/4019095.stm.

Grossman, Lev. "Iran's Protests: Why Twitter Is the Medium of the Movement," June 17, 2009. www.time.com/time/printout/0,8816,1905125,00.html.

Hampton, Keith, Lee Rainie, Weixu Lu, Maria Dwyer, Inyoung Shin, and Kristen Purcell. "Social Media and the 'Spiral of Silence.'" *Pew Research Center, Washington, DC* Pewinternet.org/2014/08/26/social-Mediaand-the-Spiral-of-Silence, 2014. http://1percent.info/wp-content/uploads/2014/12/2014-Social-Media-and-the-Spiral-of-Silence.pdf.

Hayek, Friedrich A. "The Use of Knowledge in Society." *American Economic Review* 35, no. 4 (1945): 519–530.

Hayes, Hannah. "What Will Nate Silver Do Next?," 2009. www.uchicago.edu/features/20090126_silver.shtml.

Hiltzik, Michael. "Susan G. Komen Foundation Discovers the Price of Playing Politics." *Los Angeles Times*. Accessed August 17, 2015. www.latimes.com/business/hiltzik/la-fi-mh-susan-g-komen-20140108-story.html.

"How a 'Denial of Service' Attack Works," February 9, 2000. http://news.cnet.com/2100-1017-236728.html.

"How to Take down an Iranian Government Website," June 14, 2009. www.dailykos.com/story/2009/6/14/742517/-How-to-take-down-an-Iranian-Government-Website.

"In New Video on Eve of Kony 2012 Day of Action, Senators Underscore Support for U.S. Efforts to Help Capture Joseph Kony| News Releases| U.S. Senator Chris Coons of Delaware." Accessed August 16, 2015. www.coons.senate.gov/newsroom/releases/release/in-new-video-on-eve-of-kony-2012-day-of-action-senators-underscore-support-for-us-efforts-to-help-capture-joseph-kony.

"Iran Blocks TV, Radio and Phones – but Web Proves More Difficult," June 15, 2009. www.guardian.co.uk/technology/2009/jun/15/iran-jamming-technology-tv-radio-internet.

"Iran Doctor Tells of Neda's Death," June 25, 2009. http://news.bbc.co.uk/2/hi/8119713.stm.

Kaminski, Margot E., and Shane Witnov. "The Conforming Effect: First Amendment Implications of Surveillance, Beyond Chilling Speech." *University of Richmond Law Review* 49 (2015). http://papers.ssrn.com/sol3/papers.cfm?abstract_id=2550385.

"Kenlayne.com (Internet Archive: Dec 14, 2001)," n.d. http://web.archive.org/web/20011214072915/http:/kenlayne.com/2000/2001_12_09_logarc.html#7775149.

Kiss, Jemima. "Google and Facebook Roll out Farsi Language Tools," June 19, 2009. www.guardian.co.uk/media/pda/2009/jun/19/google-facebook.

Kliff, Sarah, and Lena H. Sun. "Planned Parenthood Says Komen Decision Causes Donation Spike." *The Washington Post*, February 1, 2012. www.washingtonpost.com/national/health-science/planned-parenthood-says-komen-decision-causes-donation-spike/2012/02/01/gIQAGLsxiQ_story.html.

Kroll, Alden. "Removing Payment," April 27, 2015. http://steamcommunity.com/games/SteamWorkshop/announcements/detail/208632365253244218.

Kuchera, Ben. "Valve launches Steam Community, perhaps a bit soon | Ars Technica," August 7, 2007. http://arstechnica.com/gaming/2007/08/valve-launches-steam-community-perhaps-a-bit-soon/.

Magazine, Kate Dailey, BBC News. "Komen and Planned Parenthood: The Pink Army Revolts." Accessed August 17, 2015. www.bbc.com/news/magazine-16865529.

Margolis, Michael, and David Resnick. *Politics as Usual: The Cyberspace "Revolution."* Thousand Oaks, CA: Sage Publications, 2000.

"Massive Censorship Accompanies Ahmadinejad 'Victory,'" June 13, 2009. www.rsf.org/Massive-censorship-accompanies.html.

"MODs and Steam • /r/gaming." *Reddit*. Accessed August 17, 2015. www.reddit.com/r/gaming/comments/33uplp/mods_and_steam/cqojx8y.

Morozov, Evgeny. "DDOS Attacks on Iran's Web-Sites: What a Stupid Idea!," June 15, 2009. http://neteffect.foreignpolicy.com/posts/2009/06/15/ddos_attacks_on_irans_web_sites_what_a_stupid_idea.

"Mousavi Officially Contests Iran Election Results," June 14, 2009. www.alarabiya.net/articles/2009/06/14/75900.html.

"NLRB Continues Aggressive Crackdown on Social Media Policies." *The National Law Review*. Accessed August 16, 2015. www.natlawreview.com/article/nlrb-continues-aggressive-crackdown-social-media-policies.

"NLRB Signs Off on Employer Social Media Policy as Legal." Accessed August 16, 2015. www.workforce.com/blogs/3-the-practical-employer/post/21288-nlrb-signs-off-on-employer-social-media-policy-as-legal.

"Overspending and Decline in Funding Force Invisible Children to Announce 2015 Closure." *Humanosphere*. Accessed August 15, 2015. www.humanosphere.org/world-politics/2014/12/overspending-decline-funding-force-invisible-children-announce-2015-closure/.

Parlock, Joe. "The first paid Skyrim mod has been pulled," April 24, 2015. www.destructoid.com/the-first-paid-skyrim-mod-has-been-pulled-290924.phtml.

Peskin, Doron. "Iranian Election Costs Millions," June 13, 2009. www.ynetnews.com/articles/0,7340,L-3730357,00.html.

Plunkett, Luke. "Steam Is 10 Today. Remember When It Sucked?," September 12, 2013. http://kotaku.com/steam-is-10-today-remember-when-it-sucked-1297594444.

Preston, Pam, Jennifer Belluck, and Gardiner Harris. "Komen Reverses Stance on Planned Parenthood Grants." *The New York Times*, February 3, 2012. www.nytimes.com/2012/02/04/health/policy/komen-breast-cancer-group-reverses-decision-that-cut-off-planned-parenthood.html.

Raymond, Eric S. "NedaNet Resource Page," n.d. www.nedanet.org.

Reinikainen, Esko. "#iranelection Cyberwar Guide for Beginners." *Networked Culture*, June 16, 2009. http://reinikainen.co.uk/2009/06/iranelection-cyberwar-guide-for-beginners/.

Reinikainen, Esko "#iranelection – Part 2 – Cyberwar Guide for Beginners," June 23, 2009. http://reinikainen.co.uk/2009/06/iranelection-part-2-the-beginners-guide-to-cyberwar/.

Ribeiro, John. "Facebook Blocked in Iran Ahead of Elections," May 25, 2009. www.pcworld.com/article/165448/facebook_blocked_in_iran_ahead_of_elections.html.

Richards, Neil M. "Dangers of Surveillance, The." *Harvard Law Rev*iew 126 (2012): 1934.

Sayah, Reza. "Ahmadinejad Denies Calling for Facebook Ban," May 25, 2009. www.cnn.com/2009/WORLD/meast/05/25/iran.ahmadinejad.facebook/index.html.

"Senate Condemns Crimes of Joseph Kony and Lord's Resistance Army| News Releases| U.S. Senator Chris Coons of Delaware." Accessed August 15, 2015. www.coons.senate.gov/newsroom/releases/release/senate-condemns-crimes-of-joseph-kony-and-lords-resistance-army.

Sennett, Richard. *Authority*. London: Faber and Faber, 1993.

Setrakian, Lara. "Iran's Pres. Candidates Recognize the Web as a Go-To to Win," May 17, 2009. http://abcnews.go.com/print?id=7605453.

Shachtman, Noah. "Activists Launch Hack Attacks on Tehran Regime." *Wired*, June 15, 2009. www.wired.com/dangerroom/2009/06/activists-launch-hack-attacks-on-tehran-regime/.

"Skyrim Mods: Why We Gave It a Shot," April 27, 2015. www.bethblog.com/2015/04/27/why-were-trying-paid-skyrim-mods-on-steam/.

"SMS Messages Rise to 110 Million a Day amid Presidential Campaigns," June 11, 2009. www.tehrantimes.com/index_View.asp?code=196452.

"State Laws About Social Media Privacy." Accessed August 17, 2015. www.ncsl.org/research/telecommunications-and-information-technology/state-laws-prohibiting-access-to-social-media-usernames-and-passwords.aspx.

"Steam Community Features Launch | The Escapist," September 17, 2007. www.escapistmagazine.com/news/view/76961-Steam-Community-Features-Launch.

"Steam Surpasses 13 Million Accounts," May 23, 2007. www.valvesoftware.com/news/?id=1050.

"Steam Workshop Now Supporting Paid Creations," April 23, 2015. http://steamcommunity.com/workshop/aboutpaidcontent/.

Stelter, Brian. "Times to Host Blog on Politics and Polls." *The New York Times*. June 3, 2010. www.nytimes.com/2010/06/04/business/media/04silver.html.

Sternbergh, Adam. "The Spreadsheet Psychic." *New York Magazine*, October 12, 2008. http://nymag.com/news/features/51170/.

Sweney, Mark. "Google Chief: Iran Can't Control the Net," June 26, 2009. www.guardian.co.uk/media/2009/jun/26/google-iran-eric-schmidt.

Tassi, Paul. "Valve's Paid 'Skyrim' Mods Are A Legal, Ethical And Creative Disaster." *Forbes*, April 24, 2015. www.forbes.com/sites/insertcoin/2015/04/24/valves-paid-skyrim-mods-are-a-legal-ethical-and-creative-disaster/.

Terdiman, Daniel. "'#CNNFAIL': Twitterverse Slams Network's Iran Absence," June 14, 2009. http://news.cnet.com/8301-17939_109-10264398-2.html.

"Top-Secret Document Reveals NSA Spied On Porn Habits As Part Of Plan To Discredit 'Radicalizers.'" *The Huffington Post*. Accessed August 16, 2015. www.huffingtonpost.com/2013/11/26/nsa-porn-muslims_n_4346128.html.

"Valve: Remove the paid content of the Steam Workshop." *Change.org*, April 23, 2015. www.change.org/p/valve-remove-the-paid-content-of-the-steam-workshop.

Wallis, David. "Komen Foundation Works to Regain Support After Planned Parenthood Controversy." *The New York Times*, November 8, 2012. www.nytimes.com/2012/11/09/giving/komen-foundation-works-to-regain-support-after-planned-parenthood-controversy.html.

Wasserman, Todd. "'KONY 2012' Tops 100 Million Views, Becomes the Most Viral Video in History." *Mashable*. Accessed August 16, 2015. http://mashable.com/2012/03/12/kony-most-viral/.

"Wieman v. Updegraff 344 U.S. 183(1952)." *Justia Law*. Accessed August 16, 2015. https://supreme.justia.com/cases/federal/us/344/183/case.html.

"Will Employers Still Ask for Facebook Passwords in 2014?" *USA TODAY*. Accessed August 16, 2015. www.usatoday.com/story/money/business/2014/01/10/facebook-passwords-employers/4327739/.

Conclusion

Two fundamental processes underlie political activity within democratic polities: elite competition and public reactivity. As this book has attempted to demonstrate, these two processes are inherently and inextricably linked together. Competition within the elite stratum serves to regulate the behavior of elite actors; elite actions which violate norms of acceptability are brought before the public eye, with the intent of eliciting a negative reaction from the public. Similarly, elite actors structure and mobilize constituencies within the public to improve their position within the competitive elite realm. In this manner, the public is inherently passive, expected to react when prompted by elites to do so.

However, the public's inherently reactive nature does not necessarily recognize such limitations. Segments of the public may react negatively to a variety of prompts, based on their own standards of the acceptability of elite actions. In such instances, the grievances of the public may become integrated into more conventional processes of elite competition (i.e. normalization). While the grievance is likely to be addressed in some manner through normalization, any resolution is ultimately structured within the elite realm. By contrast, public grievances that do not become integrated into normal politics may lead to elite constraint. In these limited scenarios, interested segments of the public identify and react to unacceptable elite actions, effectively punishing the offending elites through one or more mechanisms of constraint.

Complicating this distinction between elite competition and elite constraint is the rise of the networked public sphere. Through technologies and practices of networked communication, individuals possess an enhanced capacity to communicate and engage in the production of information and cultural goods in a manner that is mostly independent of elite domination. This communicative-productive capacity creates a space between the exclusive elite and non-differentiated mass layers of the social whole, in which communities of shared interest can emerge from the public, and act in more or less organized efforts. The existence of such intermediate publics has served to generally intensify both elite competition and elite constraint. Clusters of interest in the intermediate public space represent partially constituted constituencies, which elite actors may attempt to mobilize and normalize. Alternatively, individuals and groups outside of the realm of "normal" politics may attempt to organize constraint efforts and seek redress on their own terms.

Within the scope of this project, the theory of elite constraint has been primarily focused on explaining elite/non-elite relations within democratic states; there may, however, be useful applications of this concept to other contexts. Despite the weakness or lack of competitive electoral systems, elites in authoritarian or partially democratic states are also subject to various mechanisms of constraint. Non-democratic leaders may not have to answer to the public, but they nonetheless have constituencies that they must answer to (e.g. opposition group leadership, military leadership). Furthermore, as citizens in authoritarian or partially democratic states have few legal and nonviolent mechanisms for articulating their grievances, violent domestic conflict or military coups represent significant threats to the regime and the overall stability of the state. If regimes in authoritarian states are willing and able, they can repress public dissent; doing so, however, often requires the maintenance of allegiances with the military and other key elites within the country. If repression is not possible, other means of channeling public reactivity must be utilized to prevent outright violent conflict.

Processes of competition and constraint, therefore, would appear to exist in authoritarian states, but in a manner that is less publically visible. Assuming all leaders must operate within some constrained boundaries, the observation of processes and mechanisms of elite constraint need not be limited to democratic states. The growing usage of social media as a tool of political organization and protest within non-democratic states, even under highly repressive regimes, suggests the contemporary relevance of this line of inquiry.

Similarly, the scope of this project has primarily looked at elite/non-elite relations within specific countries. As briefly mentioned in Chapter 2, however, elite actors and institutions may gain or lose symbolic capital through relationships with elites in other nations. With this in mind, processes of elite competition and elite constraint may extend beyond national borders, introducing the possibility of constraint efforts emerging from transnational contexts. Such transnationalization becomes further relevant as networked communications facilitate greater communication between populations and the emergence of shared norms.

One potential example of such internationalized constraint efforts is the #BringBackOurGirls campaign in Nigeria. On April 14, 2014, the Islamic militant group Boko Haram kidnapped more than 270 Nigerian school girls from the Chibok boarding school in northeastern Nigeria. The news of the abduction sparked a local and global movement to pressure key players, such as the Nigerian government, the United States, Canada, the UK, and South Africa, to take greater actions against Boko Haram and to work to rescue the captured girls. While the movement has not been considered a great success, as the school girls have not been recovered and Boko Haram has continued to abduct women and girls, the social media movement has led to greater awareness of the issue and prompted the Nigerian government to take more aggressive action. Between April and May 2015, the Nigerian military rescued over 500 women and girls from capture.[1] This brief example illustrates the potential power of the emergence of intermediate publics in transnational contexts. What is particularly interesting for such examples is the development of symbolically effective commitments across national and cultural contexts. How and when such commitments develop among individuals, and whether or not they are recognized by elites as constituencies capable of making valid claims are highly relevant considerations for an increasingly interconnected public realm.

Note

1 "234 More Women, Children Rescued, Nigerian Says—CNN.com." "Nigeria Army Rescues Nearly 300 Females from Boko Haram—Al Jazeera English."

References

"Nigeria Army Rescues Nearly 300 Females from Boko Haram." *Al Jazeera English*. April 29, 2015. www.aljazeera.com/news/2015/04/nigerian-army-rescues-200-girls-boko-haram-camps-150428195337887.html.

Purefoy, Christian, and Ralph Ellis. "Nigeria: 234 More Women, Children Rescued." *CNN*. May 4, 2015. www.cnn.com/2015/05/01/africa/nigeria-boko-haram-hostages-rescued/.

Index

active consumption 57–9, 74–7
authority 61–4; decline of 105–7

blogs 18, 68–73
buzz 76–78

capital: forms of 31–2; cultural 32–4; economic 32–5, 65–7; social 32–6; symbolic 34–7, 42–9
chilling effects 104
citizen journalism 19
class: political 7–9; economic 36, 46–7
communicative activity 56–61, 68
constraint 30; economic 44–5; institutional 44; physical 42–4; social 45–7; practicability of 47–9

elite-liberalism 9
elite-realism 5–8
elites: public elite layer 59–67; multipolar competition 31, 61
expertise 18–20

general public 59–65, 71–9

influence 61–64; *see also* authority
intermediate public 59–68, 74–7; communicative activity of 57–61, 70–3; *see also* general public
Iranian Election 107–111

journalism, social responsibility theory of 9–10
junk thought 17–21; *see also* authority, decline of

Kony 2012 95–7

Networked public sphere 52–6
normalization 92
National Security Agency (NSA) 104

Obergefell v. Hodges (2015) 39–41

privacy 103–5
public: demands of 89–91; reactivity 1–2, 89–93
public opinion: problems of 6–8; fragmentation of 21–4; reflexive consideration of 10–16, 23–4

stratification 56–8
Susan G. Kommen Foundation 98–9

triggering event 89–92; *see also* public reactivity

vaccination-autism controversy 20–1, 72–3
Valve Corporation 99–103
voting 6–8